Bullish Thinking

Bullish Thinking

THE ADVISOR'S GUIDE TO SURVIVING AND THRIVING ON WALL STREET

Alden Cass
Brian F. Shaw
Sydney LeBlanc

WILEY

John Wiley & Sons, Inc.

Published by John Wiley & Sons, Inc., Hoboken, New Jersey.
Published simultaneously in Canada.

Photo credits: Photo of Alden Cass, page xv, copyright © Chris Casaburi, all rights reserved. Photo of Brian F. Shaw, page xvi, by Ian Leith. Photo of Sydney LeBlanc, p. xvii, by James Kydd.

Limit of Liability/Disclaimer of Warranty: While the publisher and author have used their best efforts in preparing this book, they make no representations or warranties with respect to the accuracy or completeness of the contents of this book and specifically disclaim any implied warranties of merchantability or fitness for a particular purpose. No warranty may be created or extended by sales representatives or written sales materials. The advice and strategies contained herein may not be suitable for your situation. You should consult with a professional where appropriate. Neither the publisher nor author shall be liable for any loss of profit or any other commercial damages, including but not limited to special, incidental, consequential, or other damages.

For general information on our other products and services or for technical support, please contact our Customer Care Department within the United States at (800) 762-2974, outside the United States at (317) 572-3993, or fax (317) 572-4002.

Wiley also publishes its books in a variety of electronic formats. Some content that appears in print may not be available in electronic formats. For more information about Wiley products, visit our Web site at www.wiley.com.

Library of Congress Cataloging-in-Publication Data:

Cass, Alden, 1975–
    Bullish thinking : the advisor's guide to surviving and thriving on Wall Street / Alden Cass, Brian F. Shaw, Sydney Leblanc.
        p.   cm.
    Includes index.
    ISBN 978-0-470-13770-3 (pbk.)
        1. Stockbrokers—Psychology.   2. Investment advisors–Psychology.
    3. Job stress.   I. Shaw, Brian F., 1948–   II. LeBlanc, Sydney, 1947–   III. Title.
    HG4621.C377   2008
    332.6'2—dc22
                                                        2008002512

Printed in the United States of America.

10 9 8 7 6 5 4 3 2 1

To the memory of my grandparents, Elizabeth and Adolph Mezei, who gave me the gift of a college education, and fostered the development of my strong work ethic and passion for life.—Alden Cass

To our families, friends, and colleagues who inspired us to take this rewarding journey, and who continue to remind us of what is meaningful at the end of our long days.—Brian F. Shaw, Sydney LeBlanc

Contents

Preface

WHY WE WROTE THIS BOOK

The daily demands you face as a financial advisor are exhausting. You are under extreme pressure to build a profitable practice, and at the same time comply with regulations that increasingly consume your precious time. The challenge to produce is unrelenting; the responsibility to your clients is uncompromising. You wear too many hats; among them are asset management expert, client service rep, technology specialist, stock analyst, PR and marketing manager, prospecting whiz, portfolio manager, teammate, psychologist, mentor, communicator, friend, confidant, time management guru, self-motivator, student, and others.

We believe *Bullish Thinking* is a book that will help you navigate through the stressful waters of your daily business. Whether you are a transaction-based broker or a fee-based financial advisor, stress looks, sounds, and feels the same—painful and potentially destructive on a personal and professional level. But what triggers the various stressors that can dangerously affect you? Among countless things that surface in your job, dealing with difficult clients, unsupportive managers, differentiating yourself from competition, and compliance with legal issues are just a few of the hard issues on your desk.

Bullish Thinking will serve as a personal resource to help you avoid and alleviate emotional distress. You will read about the problems, and learn the solutions that will help you return to the top of your game. The hard-hitting true stories illustrate the potential threats to your mental health, identify your problems, and outline the process of getting help. The in-depth case studies and real-life examples exemplify the challenges you face, and how they can lead to emotional breakdowns. We identify skills and strategies, including Bullish Thinking exercises, which teach mastery over the volatility and unpredictability of your job. This book also shows you how to manage and balance your personal life while working in this ever-changing industry.

You will discover immediate solutions for short- and long-term help. We, authors Dr. Brian F. Shaw, one of the developers of Cognitive-Behavioral Therapy, and Dr. Alden Cass, specialize in working with financial services executives suffering from job burnout and *behavioral paralysis,* or depression. We offer a variety of ways for individuals to proactively reduce their job stress through proven techniques, including the Bullish Thinking strategies designed by Dr. Cass, which are an important theme throughout the book.

It also underscores the importance of emotional discipline in the face of potential indulgences, emotional highs, and crushing defeats. Bullish Thinking is an easy, practical, and palatable way of teaching the cognitive therapy skills introduced to the world of psychology by Dr. Brian Shaw. Dr. Cass pioneered research on brokers' and traders' behavior, and counsels those in distress.

Who Should Read This Book

Financial advisors, stockbrokers, investment bankers, traders, financial planners, wealth managers, investment management consultants, wholesalers, and others, will all benefit from this book. Bank brokers, insurance planners, and professionals working at financial supermarkets, who are in emotional distress on the job, will also be helped by the book and its Bullish Thinking strategies and case study solutions. We also believe that spouses, partners, and significant others of financial professionals will benefit, as the book will help open dialogues with their loved ones working in the industry.

The bottom line is: If emotional distress is not addressed, it is entirely possible there may be adverse or harmful consequences to you in your professional and personal life. Here's a case in point: Our research* indicates that "stockbrokers are not using effective coping skills for the purpose of alleviating their work-related stress, and consequently, are developing the debilitating symptoms of burnout, anxiety, and depression. It is our contention that negative personal outcomes will be associated with these mental health concerns, and

---

*Alden Cass, John Lewis, Ed Simco, "Casualties of Wall Street: An Assessment of the Walking Wounded," Catalyst Strategies Group, catsg.com/casualties.asp.

will consequently lead to negative organizational outcomes such as absenteeism and a decreased quality of life for employees and their families. Also, if the early warning signs of burnout, depression, and anxiety continue to remain unnoticed by stockbrokers as well as their employers, their overall productivity and commitment to the organization may wane over time, leading to an increase in turnover. This may cost brokerage houses additional money for training replacement brokers who will more than likely suffer the same fate as their predecessors."

That being said, we believe our research, and our ongoing experience of working with financial advisors (and their managers), lends credence to the importance of preventing mental and physical illness from infringing upon the lives of these individuals.

The ultimate goal of this book is to generate awareness and a better understanding of clinical depression (feeling depressed is not something to feel shame about), as well as help you better understand your personal battles to better combat the emotional demons that may be standing between you and a fulfilled life and a thriving business. *Bullish Thinking* will help you achieve your own personal nirvana—a place of contentment, financial success, and emotional stability.

ALDEN CASS
BRIAN F. SHAW
SYDNEY LEBLANC

Acknowledgments

A labor of love, a team of dedicated professionals breathed life into this book and watched over it until it became a reality. We would like to thank this group of individuals for their tireless work and exceptional guidance throughout the entire process. Special thanks go to Marnie Shaw, a dedicated rookie in this business, for her wisdom and guidance. Thank you to Miriam and Renny Cass for teaching the values of persistence, courage, and love; and to Joe Santoro and Al Bergman for taking a chance on our project. We would also like to thank Diane Bartoli of Artist Literary Group and Lorin Rees of the Helen Rees Agency for their initial input and feedback when the book was still a concept. Our deep appreciation goes out to our team at John Wiley & Sons: Editorial Director Pamela van Giessen, for believing in the project, Associate Editor Jennifer MacDonald, Editorial Assistant Kate Wood, and Senior Production Editor Mary Daniello, for their excellent direction and handling of our manuscripts and for making our project a reality. Thanks to Mary Welsch for hours of transcribing and proofreading, making our chapters flow smoothly. Thank you Gil, Ernie, Montgomery, and Pookie for the silent comfort you brought to us.

Our most important thanks goes to our readers, the hard-working advisors and managers, who face each day not knowing which stresses and problems will meet them head on, but who, nonetheless, accept the challenges with fierce determination. We hope you find this book meaningful and that it will help you through periods of emotional distress, guiding you back to better productivity, more happiness, and a clear balance in your personal and professional life. Thank you for allowing us to know you, work with you, and help you.

A. C.
B. F. S.
S. L.

About the Authors

Dr. Alden Cass is a licensed clinical psychologist and performance enhancement coach in New York City. He is the President of Catalyst Strategies Group, a team of psychologists and performance coaches specializing in coaching financial services executives to become more productive and disciplined during market downturns and other stressful times. He works with both individual advisors and teams to overcome their skill deficits and to hone their strengths. He is a consultant for branch managers on Wall Street to help improve upon the performance and problematic behaviors of the branches' top producers. Dr. Cass conducted the nation's first clinical investigation in 25 years on the mental health of Wall Street stockbrokers. His astonishing findings were presented at both international and national research conventions and have received a tremendous amount of attention from the business and financial trade media.

Dr. Cass teamed up with the Securities Industry Association after the World Trade Center attacks of September 11, 2001, to create a symposium that targeted the coping skills of Wall Street executives. He presented his Bullish Thinking paradigm to executives to help them deal with depression, burnout, and grief. He later developed "Bullish Thinking and Subtle Sales Training" workshops presented at the Investment Management Consultant Association (IMCA), the Money Management Institute (MMI), the London Bullion Market Association convention, and the Wall Street Branch Managers Meeting, held at the Federal Reserve Bank in New York City.

Dr. Cass's coaching and profiling services are currently being used by various mutual funds as a value-added service that is delivered to the top broker-dealers nationwide. Dr. Cass sits on the board of the National Association of Investment Professionals and is a Research Committee member of the Financial Services Policy Institute. He is on the advisory board for a not-for-profit charity called FM World Charities, which focuses on preventative medicine initiatives for those less fortunate. He writes two weekly columns for The Street.com, a monthly Internet column called "The Mental Edge" for *Trader Monthly*, and a bimonthly column for *On Wall Street* magazine.

In his practice, he has spearheaded a campaign to support the wives and significant others of high-powered executives through his new weekly group, "The Wall Street Wives Club," and has developed a "Divorced Male Executive Support Group." He has also initiated a new research project focusing on empowering female investors while helping advisors understand how to cater to this existing target population.

 **Dr. Brian F. Shaw** is one of the originators of applied cognitive-behavioral psychology for clinical practice, the performance of elite athletes, creativity, health promotion, and coping with significant illness. He is an expert on how the mind works, how it gets derailed, and how to get it back on track. More important, he understands how people refresh their thinking to gain new perspectives on their life, their world, and their future.

He is the principal of BFS Consulting, a sports and entertainment consulting firm based in Toronto, Canada. As one of the developers of Cognitive-Behavioral Therapy (CBT), a psychological treatment for depression, anxiety, and substance abuse, Dr. Shaw has adapted this technology to help those suffering from serious medical illness (cancer, heart disease, eating disorders, pain syndromes, and transplantation). Over the past 15 years he has taken this research and adapted it to the everyday world, where people strive for health and peace of mind.

Dr. Shaw has developed a cognitive-behavioral approach to help individuals in the financial sector manage the demands of a career in their high-stress industry. He has counseled brokers, securities litigators, traders, and others on Wall Street for more than 20 years.

He developed, with Bruce Ferguson at the Hospital for Sick Children in Toronto, Canada, a province-wide initiative to help children and youth with mental health and addiction. This work has affected mental health, juvenile justice, and educational approaches to children and youth.

In sports, Dr. Shaw is well known for his work as the co-director of the NHL/NHLPA Substance Abuse and Behavioral Health Program. He also co-directs the behavioral health program for Major League Soccer (MLS/MLSPA). He is responsible for the educational program for all NHL and MLS players. Dr. Shaw is the psychologist for the Toronto Blue Jays and several other professional and Olympic-level athletes. He was recently a featured speaker at the player development forum hosted by the NBA, NFL, and the NHL on the topic "Managing Anxiety in Athletes" and at the 2007 seminar hosted by the Los Angeles Police Department (LAPD) on "Teen Addiction."

Scientifically, Dr. Shaw is one of the 50 highest-impact authors in psychology. He is the author, with Paul Ritvo and Jane Irvine, of *Addiction and Recovery for Dummies* (Wiley, 2004) and *Cognitive Therapy of Depression* (Guilford Press, 1979, with Aaron Beck, John Rush, and Gary Emery).

He is a professor at the University of Toronto. Dr. Shaw received his Ph.D. in Clinical Psychology at the University of Western Ontario in 1975 following a B.S. degree at the University of Toronto.

Sydney LeBlanc is a 30-year financial services industry veteran, journalist, author, and publisher. She was the co-founder and editor-in-chief of *Registered Representative* magazine, the nation's first trade magazine for stockbrokers in 1976. Later, as editor-in-chief, she led the development of *Securities Industry Management* magazine, the first publication for branch managers.

Sydney helped launch and promote the Institute for Certified Investment Management Consultants (now IMCA) in the mid-1980s. A writer for such industry organizations as the Money Management Institute, International Association of Advisors in Philanthropy, and Success Continuing Education, LLC, she is also a writing coach and marketing consultant for industry trainers, financial advisors, broker-dealers, and money managers. Sydney is the author of *Legacy: The History of Separately Managed Accounts*; *Wealth Management Teams*; *Independent Business Ownership*; and the co-author of *Streetwise Investor*, *The Wealth Factor*, *The World of Money Management*; *Happily Ever After*, *Stop and Think*; and *PR Savvy for the Financial Professional*.

She is the recipient of several awards for her work, including the Ozzie Award for Excellence in Design, the *FOLIO:* Magazine Editorial Excellence Award for *Securities Industry Management* magazine, the 2007 Managed Accounts Pioneer award from the Money Management Institute, and First Place for Signed Editorial from the American Society of Business Press Editors. Her articles have appeared in *On Wall Street, Broker/Dealer, Financial Advisor, Global Investing*, and *Research* magazines, among others.

Co-director of Fisher LeBlanc Group, a financial publishing, marketing, and communications firm, she also is the managed accounts editor for *Financial Advisor* magazine and consulting editor for *Senior Consultant News Journal*. Sydney is an officer and board member of the Washington, D.C.–based Wealth Advisor Institute and is actively involved on the Marketing and Communications committee. She is also on the board of the National Association of Investment Professionals and is a Research Committee member of the Financial Services Policy Institute.

Bullish Thinking

Introduction

You live with constant uncertainty. You ride the wild, frenetic, and unpredictable market fluctuations every day and the pressure for you to master the ups and downs is beyond comprehension. You are the first in the line of fire, having to answer to disgruntled clients when money is lost or not growing fast enough. Life in the office becomes all about capturing more assets, marketing yourself, organizing seminars, asking for referrals, keeping up to date on regulations, staying in compliance, pleasing your branch manager, learning new products, and staying current with continuing education requirements. All that and your registered assistant just quit because she said you were becoming impossible to work with.

To compensate for the many things out of your control, you inevitably will try to assert control over one of the few things you *can* dominate—your emotions. Having control over your feelings is the only aspect of your life you may feel capable of predicting, right? And you *certainly* don't want your emotions or feelings to show (as evidenced by the predominantly male culture of Wall Street, which makes it almost impossible for an advisor to reveal feelings). Showing fear, anxiety, sadness, or uncertainty would be to render yourself powerless; you would appear incompetent or weak; you would lose the respect of your colleagues and your manager. Right? But it is this constant pressure to control and conceal emotions, coupled with the unyielding stresses of the profession that promotes depersonalization (emotional numbing), alcohol and drug use, and promiscuity—all behaviors that serve as an escape from the reality of the daily challenges. These attempts to cope or distract yourself are detrimental to your physical health and work performance because they mask warning signs of burnout, anxiety, and depression. And, you may not even realize you are suffering until you sober up or come out from under the fog and your career is on the line. The damage to your job, physical health, or family often occurs before you realize you need to seek help.

Do you find you are asking yourself these types of questions:

> Why am I flying off the handle at every turn? What is making me so intolerant at work, at home? Why do I feel the need to escape, or anesthetize myself? How many drinks constitute a drinking problem? How come it takes an hour of tossing and turning before I can fall asleep? How come I can never sit still in a meeting? Should I see a doctor, get some medication? Should I quit or change jobs? Why do I feel like a failure even though I have a better-than-average income?

If you are struggling with these types of issues, you are not alone. The results of the study, "Casualties of Wall Street: An Assessment of the Walking Wounded" (developed and presented by Dr. Alden Cass as the first research of its kind about Wall Street brokers), revealed for the first time a world of suffering among brokers and advisors. Twenty-three percent of the brokers surveyed were diagnosed with clinical depression and 38 percent had mild-to-moderate symptoms. This finding is alarming because the incidence of clinical depression in males in the United States is approximately only 8 percent, according to National Institute of Mental Health statistics. A majority of the sample experienced significant levels of anxiety, emotional exhaustion, and burnout. Furthermore, brokers reported abusing alcohol and other substances such as cocaine, amphetamines, marijuana, Ritalin, and Ecstasy. They also used sex as well as promiscuity, to cope with their unrelenting stress.

The widely held traditional belief about successful brokers and advisors used to be "You will feel good if you make money." But the study showed that belief to be incorrect. In fact, the opposite was true! Successful brokers were the most mentally, or emotionally, disturbed. They were the most depressed, most burnt-out, and the most exhausted. And the highest earners used the most drugs and experienced "depersonalization." "Casualties of Wall Street" revealed a generation of brokers trading their mental health for money and affluence.

The study discovered that the highest earners, the most successful brokers, are the most troubled. But they're making money, right?

Not for long. In an eight-month follow-up survey, nearly 25 percent of the brokers who made the most money were no longer employed by their firms. They had been fired, changed jobs, or just burned out and dropped off the radar screen. While they might have been riding a successful wave, their earning potential for the long haul was hampered by their need to distance themselves from experiencing painful internal emotions such as disgust, guilt, anger, remorse, shame, and inferiority.

As you read through the pages of this book, you and other courageous brokers needing help will quickly identify with colleagues who may share the same fears, thoughts, problems, and insecurities. You will discover you may need help on a professional level, and doing so is no longer a stigma. Demystifying the taboos of mental and emotional health will help you (and others) get over the hurdles keeping you from achieving emotional health and peace of mind.

Obviously, this is not a book about the glory of making money. Nor is it a book about the technical or mechanical strategies involved in investing. It's not about motivation, selling, prospecting, or secrets of creative visualization. *Bullish Thinking: The Advisor's Guide to Surviving and Thriving on Wall Street* teaches brokers and advisors that they don't have to remain passive participants in their stressful and volatile environments. You can learn to recognize the warning signals associated with under-the-radar psychological stressors that manifest as symptoms of job burnout and depression. We introduce practical and proactive Bullish Thinking strategies that Dr. Alden Cass uses in clinical practice with brokers and advisors, as well as those techniques pioneered by Dr. Brian F. Shaw in cognitive-behavioral therapy. Bullish Thinking solutions will help you manage the daily volatility and stress of work without making you feel like you're a patient on a psychiatrist's couch.

It is our goal—no, it is our responsibility—to teach you the warning signals and dangers of depression, to uncover the myths, to offer practical solutions, and to lead you back to a healthful emotional and physical state of mind. And we want to do this in a nonthreatening, empathic, and positive manner. So, we are offering you positive ways of coping with the numerous challenges you and your fellow advisors face on the job; ways that allow changes in patterns of thinking and behaving; ways that provide relief, which will result in the achievement of a healthy mindset. Our wish is to encourage advisors like yourself to seek the coaching or counseling you may need to improve your lives and businesses and those who might not otherwise come forward to ask for help. The payback for everyone is the industry will see that psychology and business can coexist.

We are dedicated to the mission of countering the misunderstanding and stigmas that we observe every day in the financial services industry. These are the conditions that we label as mental illness and addiction, but that we know even better as human tragedy. We are committed to preventing the mental and physical casualties proliferating in the industry today.

This book is the first step in that direction.

1

The Hard Issues on Your Desk

WHAT IS DRIVING YOU TO DESTRUCTION?

At 9 P.M., at the end of a hectic 12-hour day, John, a successful 38-year-old million-dollar producer at a major wirehouse in downtown Manhattan, closed the door to his office, locked it, and took the elevator to the thirty-sixth floor of his office building. Despondent over recent losses his clients had suffered in the market over the past year, John had been short-tempered and adversarial with colleagues as well as with his branch manager, and threatened to leave the industry on more than one occasion. He had a long history of mood swings, which seemed to only worsen when he was faced with difficult events at work. This business was crushing him. Not only had he let his clients down, but, just as important, he had let himself down.

When the elevator door closed behind him, he took the stairs to the roof where he breathed in the cool night air. With an empty stare, he slowly made his way across the roof with a purposeful pace. John walked to the roof's ledge, looked out across the looming dark city skyline, mumbled a prayer for his wife and children, closed his eyes . . . and jumped.

The next day, it was business as usual on Wall Street.

The Reality of Life on the Street—and in the Office

You already know the reality: Wall Street attracts men and women who are driven toward extremes, who crave a challenge, who must win against all odds, and above all, who can push themselves to the limit and beyond. Wall Street is for the strong-willed.

Like John . . .

Tragically, John was consumed by—and succumbed to—the stresses of the Street. The demands advisors face are unending. But the culture and values of Wall Street firms begin and end with the bottom line. They are under extreme pressure to create and build profits and, at the same time, to comply with regulations that increasingly consume the time of middle and upper management. The demands on advisors to produce and build assets are unrelenting; the onus on branch managers to supervise is uncompromising.

Whether you are a transaction-based broker or a fee-based financial advisor, stress looks, sounds, and feels the same—painful and potentially destructive on a personal and a professional level. But what, with the exception of market downturns and uncertainties, triggers the various stressors that can dangerously affect you? Let's take a look at some of the hard issues on your desk.

You wear many hats. Among them are: asset management expert, customer service rep, technology specialist, stock analyst, PR and marketing manager, prospecting whiz, portfolio manager, teammate, counselor, mentor, communicator, friend, party promoter, confidant, time management guru, self-motivator, student, and on and on.

How many hats do you wear? Are they on this list? Is it any surprise, then, that you and other hard-working professionals face significant daily stresses? Here are a few typical examples of everyday stressors:

- Unhappy, difficult, or bothersome clients
- Transitioning from commissions to fee-based business
- Transition from working solo to working on a team
- Conflicts or bad communication with branch manager
- No support or recognition or validation from the manager
- Keeping up with the alpha dogs—competition with colleagues on the leaderboard
- Competitive environment with producing manager
- Compliance and legal issues

- Stress of capturing more assets; bringing on more clients
- Market downturns
- Merging a practice or establishing a team
- Data and information overload
- Professional development; continuing education
- Balancing family life, social life, and work life
- Addiction issues
- Conflicts and separations within a team

These examples, coupled with the housing market crisis and events of recent years (the September 11th tragedy, the Iraq war, the tech bubble burst, and so on), create extreme and unrelenting anxiety under which even the most strong-willed brokers and advisors may buckle. Buried feelings begin to surface. First, a feeling of helplessness emerges ("There's nothing I can do to change it"), which may lead to hopelessness ("This is never going to end") and, eventually, a deep sense of worthlessness ("I can't handle it anymore; I can't take the heat").

Let's take a look at a typical advisor experiencing some of the stressors listed here. We'll call him "the Iceman."* Characteristically, the Iceman could be anywhere from 30 to 60 years old, having a tenure in the financial services industry anywhere from five to 25 years. He is aptly named because he has turned off his ability to emote, to give, to allow others to see how he is feeling. He has become numb to his own feelings, and regardless of whether he is challenged by difficult clients, market downturns, unresponsive managers, or otherwise, his stress is real and he reacts to it by shutting down.

The Iceman has trouble showing such feelings as anger, frustration, disillusionment, and worry. During times of heightened depression or anxiety, this individual can mask his symptoms and feelings by working longer hours, spending more time playing (or obsessing) with stimulation toys like PDAs, digital music players, cell phones, video games, pornography, and so on. Icemen distract themselves from their emotional pain or frustration and, ultimately, they also lose their ability to notice when *other* people are in distress. This causes problems with clients and prospects, and plays a large part in creating distress within marriages or other relationships.

---

*The Iceman is used in a gender-neutral sense. This individual can be a male or a female.

As an Iceman, you mentally bow out of the competitive challenge at work, and resign yourself to inactivity. You want to numb or distract yourself from stressors, and, oftentimes, this numbness is achieved by using alcohol, marijuana, prescription drugs like Vicodin, Oxycontin, Xanax, or prescription stimulants like Adderall or Ritalin, just to get through the day. The substance abuse and the stimulation toys contribute to the distraction and the lack of self-awareness, which leads to the continuation of the pervasive detachment from almost everything that is important in your life. This can be an invasive situation with tentacles winding their way into various areas of your life, eventually strangling you.

The Iceman feels he is not gaining any ground or accomplishing anything positive, so he begins to feel useless. Making changes to the work environment or to the home environment seems futile. An analogy would be a person trying to run in quicksand: struggling, he can't get anywhere, sinking deeper the more he tries. For example, you may irrationally perceive that talking to your branch manager about your problems (lack of support, lack of resources designated for you) won't help matters, and that your manager is either too busy to listen, or he doesn't care. Or you may have a client who needs a lot of hand-holding—one who may get upset about drops in her portfolio performance, and you just can't face her. You can't manage her expectations anymore, and maybe you just don't care.

As an Iceman, you become a product of overinvesting in work, and not enough in your family life or mental and emotional wellness. This is a consistent problem throughout the industry because it's very hard to walk that tightrope between doing both, but advisors often need someone to hold them accountable for what they are doing. You forget, once you're comfortable in a marriage or a relationship, for example, that it still needs tending. So when things are going poorly in your personal life, you tend to jump into work but continue to dwell about an unresolved conflict or issue at home that you either know how to deal with but don't want to deal with, or are afraid to ask for help about it from a teammate or colleague or your branch manager.

The real issue is that Icemen feel they can't even ask their branch manager how to solve a problem with their wife, because that's not the branch manager's job, and they're afraid to ask for someone else's advice out of fear of appearing weak. After the September 11th tragedy, one of us (Dr. Cass) was volunteering on Wall Street at various brokerage houses. He had interviewed and counseled two advisors who were sitting at desks next to each other. They had worked together for more than two years and they each told Dr. Cass (in confidence) that they were suffering from symptoms of Post-Traumatic Stress Disorder as a result of witnessing the World Trade Center buildings collapse, and had never talked with anyone about it before. One of the advisors said he was having flashbacks every time he walked toward the subway; he thought he was seeing planes crashing into buildings. While he was walking to the subway, he'd break into panic attacks and start sweating profusely. He could not get on a train; he had to arrange for alternate transportation to work every day from Brooklyn. The other advisor said that he had not been sleeping for weeks because he was having nightmares about September 11th.

Now, mind you, both of these advisors were also friends. Dr. Cass asked them both (individually) and they acknowledged that they had not told each other about their symptoms. They were working very close together, every day, sharing business experiences, managing other people's money. But not sharing personal experiences that were interfering with their performance. That's a classic example of how events and issues within your personal life affect your physical well-being, your mental well-being, and manifest themselves in your professional life.

An Action-Oriented Solution: Introducing
Bullish Thinking

Our mind is a powerful weapon against the job stresses we all face every day at work. We often do not know, however, how to harness it while we are up against deadlines or when we are forced to make tough decisions after having endured a failure or setback in our performance. The key question for any advisor, broker, planner, trader, or manager is: *"What is it that sets me apart from my colleagues when faced with a setback or a challenge?"*

The quick and dirty answer is: An action-oriented, self-monitoring intervention that allows individuals to transcend any work stressor with perseverance and gives them a sense of control over their jobs. We call it *Bullish Thinking.*

We explain and explore this positive intervention in depth in Chapter 3, but first let's examine the symptoms and the roots of the emotional challenges you and others may be facing through the hard issues on your desk. We help you understand your personal battles and learn to combat the emotional demons that may be standing between you and a fulfilled life and a thriving business. You will learn that Bullish Thinking will allow you to achieve your own personal nirvana—a place of contentment, financial success, and emotional stability.

We also introduce, Ned, our desperate advisor who exhibits numerous symptoms of burnout, anxiety, and depression, and how Bullish Thinking helped him get back on the bull.

CHAPTER 2

Emotional Issues

THE RED FLAGS OF DISCONTENT, DISTRESS, DESPAIR

Recognizing the symptoms of emotional distress is the first step in preventing the escalation of an underlying emotional problem. As we illustrated in the example of the Iceman in the previous chapter, he was suffering from various ailments, burnout being one of them.

Burnout is one stage before it may become depression. Let's look at it as a continuum. If normal, everyday stress is about 5 on a 1–10 scale (10 being the most stressful), and most people perform at an optimal level at a 5 or 6, we can safely assume that advisors are forced to work very hard at keeping their anxiety level from reaching a level of 7 or above. (See Figure 2.1.)

If the stress, frustration, or disillusionment facing the advisor is not corrected or challenged, and subsequently brought down to levels that are in alignment with reality, then burnout rears it head. And it can be ugly. If you are experiencing burnout, or have a genetic predisposition toward depression, and it is left unchecked, you can begin to experience prominent symptoms of major depression, which may require medication and intensive therapy.

Some of the initial symptoms of burnout are abrupt episodes of agitation, fatigue, and poor concentration. It can feel like being trapped in quicksand, and an individual often perceives any efforts to change his work situation as being futile. You may suddenly become irritable, insensitive to others' feelings, snappy, and overreactive to

RAGE & FURY

FRUSTRATION

MILD IRRITATION

COMPETITIVE

Figure 2.1   Continuum of Anxiety and Burnout

even the most trivial of things. Depending on what the perceived threat is, you may try to hold it together for the sake of your clients and, perhaps, your branch manager, and then dump on everyone else, including your spouse and family members, friends, and significant others. Advisors who are skilled at projecting confidence will do everything in their power to keep their frustrations from their clients and others. It's rare when an advisor will openly admit to uncertainty, fear, worry, or anxiety. It's uncommon and a well-kept secret.

Self-defeating thoughts and pessimism about their future will hamper an individual's performance, whether he is working on the Street or playing in a sports arena. For advisors, the heat is on every day. In sports, it's game seven of the championship series. In law, it's the high profile case. In the world of finance, it's hunting the big elephants and bringing them on as clients. It's managing clients' life savings, building and preserving their wealth. At the same time, they are trying to make a living, building their book of business, capturing more assets, targeting the high net worth investor, and staying in compliance.

What wrecks the train for these advisors are the variables they can't control, or don't anticipate. Volatile markets, terrorism, corporate scandals, threat of inflation, foreign crises, divorce, family tragedy, and war are obvious examples. Inevitably, as advisors continue down their career paths, capture larger assets, manage money— whether retail or institutional—many tend to think of their clients as numbers—or situations or problems—and the day-to-day business of working with them becomes less personal and more technical.

In essence, advisors become depersonalized, creating an emotional distance between themselves and their clients. They begin treating their clients as though they were useful only for monetary gain so they can avoid experiencing painful emotions like sadness, frustration, worry, or anger. Much like a nightclub promoter begins to count heads at the door to anticipate his take for the night, to advisors, their clients at times similarly become just heads. High achievers like to solve problems, the bigger the better. They love the challenge, the action. Once they have landed a client and the challenge has been overcome, however, some advisors have a tendency to move them to the back of their priority list. Consequently, their servicing mentality will only apply to novel and potential clients. But these very characteristics can make it difficult to understand the thoughts, feelings, and needs of others, including those of their colleagues and family members.

So, what do we see? We see advisors beginning to respond to the numbers, or the situation, instead of to the client.

Are You a Perfectionist?

Dr. Cass pioneered one of the first clinical investigations on the mental health of Wall Street advisors. One of the most interesting data points generated within the course of his investigation was that 96 percent of his respondents reported that they were extremely critical of themselves for their mistakes. We have also noted anecdotally in our coaching practices that a clear majority of our clients have this similar overlapping thought process about the quality of their work. It seems that Type A individuals can relate to experiencing this intense desire to be perfect and be self-critical of their mistakes. Although there are five advisor mindsets that we have recognized with divergent characteristics and traits, it seems that this style of perfectionism overlaps among the group of five styles. The five advisor mindsets are not completely mutually exclusive, as there will always be some shared behavioral tendencies across the spectrum of individuals such as this one seems to be.

Not surprisingly, many advisors, by nature, are hard-driving individuals who follow an all-or-nothing philosophy. It's either win or lose—they can't stomach the gray area. This is an industry, though, with a lot of gray areas: uncertainty, low predictability, irregularity, and volatility. And it will never change. Many advisors have difficulty handling these factors and, as a result, find themselves in an excruciatingly challenging work environment, mainly because they do not have the ability or the tools to remedy the particular situation they may be facing.

The remedy is to be proactive and realistic, especially with clients. During serious market downturns, advisors are expected to be in touch with clients, even though it might be paralyzing to think about because these contacts are usually very emotional. Markets are cyclical; most investors expect to ride these things out, especially those who are investing for the longer term. And the proactive aspect of the relationship is crucial. As an advisor, you already know which clients are going to react emotionally when markets drop or if their portfolio performance isn't right on target. Knowing that is half the battle. You will encourage the clients and reframe the negative scenarios into more realistic ones over the long term.

Part of your own battle when you are stressed and anxious, of course, is to keep your thoughts rational and adaptive about the upsetting situation, reminding yourself that setbacks are a part of life and are temporary, and many times the challenges will eventually right themselves with your proactivity. You need to challenge yourself to get rid of your irrational tendencies to be, for example, a perfectionist or to try to control the uncontrollable. Everyone makes mistakes. Everyone. You may want to try using the Anchor Technique.

Anchoring is a well-accepted psychological technique whereby a word, a phrase, or a theme is repeated. It is repeated from the same spot, with the same gestures, with the same facial expressions, the same tone of voice, and with the same mannerisms. One example of anchoring that many of us can remember was done by the late, great Jack Benny, who had a certain way of folding his arms, putting his chin into his hand, and saying, with some exaggeration, "Well . . ." Pretty soon, he was getting laughs without even saying the word, and eventually did not even need to put his chin into his hand. He simply used part of the routine and the anchor worked. Anchoring causes an association of the subject matter anchored with an emotional response that is initiated by the repeated use of the anchoring technique. In essence, it communicates our theme on an emotional level with a greater impact.

Using the Anchor Technique Successfully

As mentioned earlier, some advisors are all-or-nothing thinkers when it comes to their perception of success or failure. They have expectations that every project or initiative they participate in must have a successful outcome. For them, second place is never an option. For example, when a rift exists between what they expected from their quarterly production and the statistical reality of their assets under management, a perfectionistic advisor can take a serious emotional hit. In this scenario, the advisor may develop self-defeating thoughts about his competence and may even see his business as being a failure. When an advisor falls into this trap, it becomes very difficult to see the real-life evidence that exists right in front of him that contradicts his crippling and maladaptive beliefs or predictions about a slip in performance. His mind has not been trained to challenge his impending negative thoughts, and, oftentimes, event-driven crises are perceived as being long-term in nature rather than short-term. We call this pattern of thinking *catastrophizing*.

In working with these overachieving advisors in practice, we have found practical ways to get them to use facts and data from their past successes for the purpose of warding off these irrational and negativistic thought patterns. Here's how to use it:

Jim, a financial advisor, came to us because he thought his business would never recover from two big accounts walking out on him within a two-month period when the markets were performing poorly. He thought that his business was finished and that new clients would be turned off to his presentation style. Jim, who was a premier advisor for six years, had experienced minor slumps like this before, but never had accounts this large taken their money elsewhere. We encouraged him to think about every time in the past six years when his business suffered and how he reacted to it. He noted that he was equally as pessimistic at those times about the future of his business. Then we focused on the reality of the longer-term outcome stemming from those negative events. He also recalled that he had picked up new accounts when he least expected to. He remembered that his best approach was to continue calling prospects and making presentations. He didn't want to "go back" but agreed that it was the best plan. In time, he felt that his business was safe. He *anchored* his thoughts back to tangible past failures, but was able to see his way out successfully. Now he could look at this bad two-month period as being nothing more than an aberration or short-term setback in his business, rather than as a mark against his competence or future potential. This therapy work is actually very difficult and needs to be practiced regularly. Jim was able to go back and use this technique many times.

These individuals have one of the most persistent patterns of thinking that you will ever see. We should repeat the *fact* that it takes discipline, work, and patience to get to this stage. Think of your worst habit and how hard it would be to change—that's what it takes!

Helpless, Hopeless, and Worthless?

Clinical depression and anxiety are relatively common syndromes that have serious negative physical, emotional, and behavioral implications. These syndromes can rob one of needed energy and pleasure, cause early morning awakening, late afternoon fatigue, and other sleep problems. There may also be a feeling of dread. They may wrack a person's nerves to the point of collapse. The core changes in thinking associated with depression are a sense of helplessness, hopelessness, and worthlessness. Let's discuss the definitions and study some examples.

Helplessness. A state of mind, defined by an inability to perceive any control over the events in one's life—and, even worse, the inability to predict when future negative events may emerge. "No matter what I do, nothing works." "I can't even see when the next wave is going to hit me!" If an advisor is in a situation when the stress is unrelenting (pretty much every day on Wall Street), he may begin to question his competence. "What am I doing? I can't compete, can't keep up. I'm getting hammered here. I don't know what to do. There is no way out of this situation." The achievements of others may make this individual feel like a total loser. "How do they keep up? How do they do it? I can't believe it! No matter what I do, I screw it up. I can't win."

These thoughts drive one's mind into a state of paralysis and shock. At this point, an advisor may retreat to a protective passive stance, lying in bed wishing that life's responsibilities would stop weighing down on him, if only for a moment. In a crippling state, the advisor is frozen, feeling sick, while the world spins past.

Now here's the real kicker. Perfectionism and the fear of failure turn into hostility. A self-hatred for being weak can drive some advisors into further despair. The highly self-critical and harshly judgmental attitude that fuels their ambition and blind courage works against them as they try to understand why they can't impose their will on the work environment. They believe that no matter what they do, they can't change or control the situation or circumstance. They know that something is wrong with them, but don't know what it is. Tragically, this scenario continues to drive these advisors down in the same way that our immune system—which is designed to fight off infection—can turn on us. Both conditions can be costly if they aren't treated effectively and quickly.

Hopelessness. Adopting a helpless stance in managing our emotional states accelerates and perpetuates a sense of hopelessness, a belief that failure and loss is inevitable, so giving up is the only course. Hopelessness is best seen as a flood of negative predictions: "I am doomed. This strategy will never work"; "Life isn't worth living; nothing ever goes right for me; I can't stand it anymore," and a feeling that we can't see anything bright in the future. Our stream of thoughts are filled with black and white words like *never, anymore, doomed,* or other examples like *always* and *impossible.* In essence, we see a gray and cloudy sky instead of the streaks of sunshine peeking through. Eventually, and at times tragically, the hopelessness merges into a state of mind where you lose time. Time actually flies by. There is no future, only the dark present, and it's filled with anxiety.

Worthlessness.   Over time, an advisor may start to ask, "Why? Why me? Why is everything going so badly?" He usually comes to one conclusion . . . that *he* is the problem. He is so tough on himself, using self-deprecating statements like "I am worthless, a loser who can't compete, can't take care of business. I am washed up, a has-been who might as well check out now. I am a piece of garbage and am flooded with my past memories of failure and loss. I'm totally useless." On occasion, individuals who feel this way may actually sabotage relationships with people they care about because they feel guilty about bringing others down with them. Furthermore, they may also avoid loved ones because they no longer feel worthy of being around them.

It hurts so badly that they ache; they physically ache with the belief that *they and they alone* are the cause of their own misfortune. There is no one else to blame. Not the manager, not the firm, not the spouse, kids, or dog. They've known it for a long time. They've been living a lie, making those they care about feel like they have brought them down. Who are they kidding? These advisors are some of the world's great imposters, right? Losers who have fooled everyone . . . right?

Do you see the power of negative thinking? It is paralyzing and gut-wrenching. There seems to be no way out, but there is! Our research has shown that this powerful triple threat to sanity of "helplessness, hopelessness, and worthlessness" (known as the Cognitive Triad*) can be beaten. It is, in fact, based on major errors in thinking and significant biochemical changes in brain chemistry. Individuals can learn how to identify this Cognitive Triad—*the sense of helplessness,*

---

*Cognitive Triad: When a depressed individual harbors negative views about the future, the self, and the world. This type of thinking is an automatic result of depression. From Aaron T. Beck, A. John Rush, Brian F. Shaw, Gary Emery, *Cognitive Therapy of Depression* (New York: Guilford Press, 1979).

hopelessness, and *worthlessness* that consumes their thinking much like fire consumes oxygen, sucking the life out of them. They can learn to combat it and defeat the thinking associated with depression and anxiety.

The Symptoms Emerge

When our job is going well, we are expansive and euphoric. We have a sense of being in control and may believe we can actually predict certain events. We start to feel invincible, almost like we have the Midas touch. Many advisors and traders begin to feel this way. Risk-taking comes more easily and their thirst for indulgences becomes insatiable. In this scenario, one must watch out for the negative consequences, both financial and personal, when "irrational exuberance" starts to appear. When things are going badly, the thinking flips, and anxiety sets in, and the blame game begins. Initially, these advisors might point the finger at everything and everyone except themselves for their failure. Blame may be placed on specific members within their team, their branch manager, or even their spouse!

After a while, these advisors begin to believe that it is, in fact, their decisions and judgments that are wrong. They have failed. The blame lies within themselves. Unfortunately, they may have already lost many friends, colleagues, and loved ones in the wake of this blaming. It is a vicious cycle perpetuated by a lack of emotional insight, and a tunnel-vision focus on achieving material wealth.

To understand it fully, it's important to know that this pattern springs from a *fear of failure.* An advisor may be afraid that if she fails, she will be exposed for her weaknesses. This type of thinking is characterized by *actual fear.* "What if I can't recover my position?" "If only I hadn't put everything on the line." "What if I lose my clients—they might see through me." "What is X going to say?"

In the healthy advisor, the thought process goes like this: "Okay, I made some serious mistakes. I screwed up. I'll accept responsibility. Everybody fails from time to time and I just have to tolerate it, get through it, and move on. This is a temporary setback, and my past performance bringing my clients returns will repeat itself this year. What can I learn from this experience? I'll be fine if I accept my mistakes and learn from them."

But what begins to happen in this situation, and with any fear, if it is not corrected, is that anxiety-based physiological symptoms surface.

Known as the "fight or flight" response, one may become aggressive or, at the very least, irritable. Muscles tense, and blood pressure goes up, the heart rate gets faster, and breathing gets shallow. This individual is ready to fight. He is waiting for the next threat or challenge to rear up so he can blast off against all comers. One can't sustain this state for very long. Adrenaline is surging through one's veins and in time, fatigue sets in. If a person remains wired, his sleep will be disrupted, perhaps with the dreaded early morning awakening (up at 3 or 4 A.M. and ready to go—this is the path to exhaustion).

These physiological symptoms are the same that advisors will experience with anxiety. Anger and anxiety have the same physiological symptoms based on the adrenaline response. The difference is that anxiety is fueled by the mindset of threat or danger, and anger has the mindset of injustice or being wronged or hurt. In both cases, the adrenaline kicks in and prepares the individual for fight or flight. This person is wired.

> *Anger.* Anger can be divided into two themes, or components (states of mind, really). The first component is *frustration*—when an individual feels stifled or restricted because he knows he has been blocked from a desired goal. "They can't do that to me—that's not fair—I won't stand by and let them screw me."
>
> *Resentment.* The second anger-driven mindset is a deep sense of having been wronged, or having been used or abused or deceived and taken advantage of. It is hard for this individual to see what role she played in the outcome. She *knows* what is going on and concludes (often erroneously) that she has been conned. It is likely she is viewing her world through distorted lenses colored by her strong emotions.

Resentment is the foundation of the blame game. This individual is so angry that she *has to understand* what went wrong. It can't be her fault—someone else did it to her. This resentful person has trouble taking responsibility. The anger really only abates once it converts to another emotional state. These angry states are maintained until the individual starts to identify and challenge the faulty and irrational thought patterns that have caused her temperature to rise, and she takes responsibility for her own actions and decisions.

The Psychological Backdrop

Human beings are very complex. It is helpful to understand that there is a connection among our feelings (angry, afraid, happy, sad, relaxed, guilty), our behaviors (avoidance, aggression, eating, sex), our brain chemistry (neurotransmitters, endorphins, immune function), *and* our thought processes (statements that we say to ourselves, and pictures and images in our minds). All automatic thoughts (ones that occur without conscious effort) are subjective reactions to life events. Some of the events are in our environment, while others are internal events (such as bodily reactions like pain or other sensations).

Second, our thinking is connected to our basic attitudes (beliefs such as, "If I don't achieve, I'm worthless" versus "I can succeed; I can handle adversity and hard times"). Our attitude is connected to our pattern of basic needs (food, water, warmth, comfort) as well as our psychological needs (achievement, affiliation, dominance, nurturance, succorance). Our basic needs are common to all humans and animals while our psychological needs vary widely.

Third, psychological needs influence decision-making and attitudes. The end result is a stream of thoughts and images in our minds that seem to develop automatically (without conscious effort). Automatic thoughts are frequently the thoughts and images associated with emotion (sadness, anger, fear). They are not planned and can come out of the blue. They relate to our judgments of ourselves ("I'm a confident person") or to the situation ("This place is frightening").

For example, let's say a fellow advisor has a strong need for achievement, dominance, and social recognition, and a low need for nurturance (caring for others) and affiliation (friendships, support). His mindset will likely reflect a "take no prisoners; damn the torpedoes, full steam ahead" attitude. This person will be goal-oriented, enjoy solving problems, and will want the credit for his achievements—all of the credit, if he can get it. He will view others as being usable and valuable only if they serve as a means to an end.

His thinking will be dominated by a need for control and by feelings of frustration. He won't tolerate sloths or fools. This person will focus on all the perks that accompany success and power. Do you think this advisor is vulnerable to emotional problems? The answer is yes. This individual is very vulnerable. The thinking under stress can break down into helplessness and agony. Let's illustrate:

Situation: "My manager dumped on me for missing my gross production goal for the month" *or* "My manager dumped on me for not meeting my goal of gathering an additional $250,000 in assets. He said I was going to have to do much better."

Responses: Automatic thoughts with associated emotions in parentheses: "He can't treat me like that" (anger). "Who does he think he is" (indignant)? "I'll show him" (furious). "I can't stand working here" (anger). "I hope he's not planning to fire me" (anxiety).

An individual's thought process about future situations can lead to a self-fulfilling prophecy. Predictions about future events can influence one's behavior, emotions, neurochemistry, and actions. This pattern of thinking is all very damaging and what we call *Bearish* (or *negative*) *Thinking*.

Curing Negative Behavior with Bullish Thinking

Bullish Thinking, a mindset posited by Dr. Cass, is a concept rooted in the principles of Cognitive-Behavioral Therapy (CBT)* as originally developed by co-author Dr. Brian F. Shaw and his colleagues. It is based on the assertion that our perceptions of stressful or negative events— whether they are bullish (positive) or bearish (negative)—actually affect how we feel and how we handle ourselves in reaction to it.

To clarify further: How we perceive a negative event is directly linked to how we handle it from a physiological, performance-based, and emotional standpoint. Also, the perception or automatic thought will affect how much we feel in control of ourselves within the context of work.

Bullish thoughts are defined as rational, mostly positive, and based on personal and historical evidence. *Bearish thoughts* are often irrational predictions, expectations, and beliefs about ourselves, others, and our future. This type of perception is often based on exaggerated or black-and-white thoughts, or overgeneralized beliefs about reality, like "I lost my client money, so I must be incompetent as a financial advisor," or "I will never overcome this bad month because of this most recent mistake."

---

*CBT is the world's most researched and evidence-based psychological therapy.

Bearish thoughts are cyclical and tend to predominate in our thinking during the course of an overwhelming week. Spending more time thinking and obsessing about recent failures or setbacks rather than about successes and achievements is a good example. This type of negative focus is very common and can be improved upon with hard work.

The helpful thing about a Bullish Thinking intervention is that it teaches the power just one realistic, positive thought has to wipe out an entire army of negative ones that often hamper our moods and productivity at work. It uses familiar Wall Street language to minimize the negative stigma associated with receiving cognitive-behavioral therapy in business. It places the responsibility on the advisor to take charge of her thought patterns to improve her productivity and emotional state. In a job where control and uncertainty can be a commodity, this level of control over some aspect of your life is usually perceived as reassuring and stabilizing. A Bullish Thinking intervention involves helping an individual to proactively manipulate her negative mood and performance states into more healthy and adaptive ones by challenging irrational and self-defeating thoughts with realistic evidence from the past or present. An intervention often involves showing an individual who is suffering, how her bearish thoughts are negatively affecting her bottom line in business or her personal relationships and supplying her with quick and practical solutions before the cycle becomes to pervasive in her life.

Before we begin discussing Bullish Thinking strategies and solutions, let's present the case of Ned, a Wall Street advisor who spiraled out of control and was on the brink of losing everything.

A Wall Street Tragedy: The Story of Ned

Veteran Wall Street reporter Landon Thomas Jr. covered depression in an in-depth article for the *New York Observer* several years ago. With the title "To Live and Throw Up on Wall Street: Diagnosing Brokers' Depression," Mr. Thomas discussed the challenges that depression caused for Wall Street professionals, including suicide, and included a case study of Ned, a broker suffering from depression and teetering on the edge of harming himself. Here is Ned's story, as told to Mr. Thomas:

Ned used to be a cold-calling machine. Smiling and dialing up to 400 prospects a day, he was a 32-year-old on a roll. He used to tell his colleagues, "I just keep throwing pitch after pitch and see what sticks. It's a numbers game." In 1999, he raked in over $500,000 in commissions and rewarded himself by buying thousand-dollar paintings and artifacts during his lunch break. He had a luxury condo in Brooklyn and a beautiful young wife who enjoyed living the high life. He was a top-gun broker early on in his career.

But now, 9 out of 10 prospects hang up on him. And most of his clients have either deserted him or have sued him. What happened?

Things started to change when he began to expect rejection on every cold call and have thoughts like, "These people don't want to hear from me," or, "I sound so stupid to the other brokers listening to my pitch." His daily contact calls were cut roughly in half as his motivation waned. He became socially withdrawn and avoided company outings and potential networking venues. His wife was less affectionate at home lately and Ned arrived home from work feeling empty inside. He felt like a shell of a man. He began to think that he needed to join a team and that this would be the quick answer to his problems. He was willing to try anything to get out of this rut.

He became short-tempered, emotionally distant, and hyper-critical of his wife for her mistakes. Communication with her was impaired and he often retired to his den after work drinking glass after glass of expensive Scotch. His mind raced and he was convinced that, "I am not a good provider anymore, I'm inadequate, and incompetent as a husband and as a broker." For Ned, the bulls stopped stampeding.

He was on the run; in retreat mode. He learned an important lesson; all that glittered wasn't gold, after all. The market turned on Ned in April 2000, just like it did for thousands of other advisors. He had plunged all of his and his clients' money into ICG Communications, Global Crossing, and Healtheon (now WebMD)—all thundering tech stocks, with profits going through the roof. When the bubble burst, stocks collapsed, he lost millions of dollars, and his life began crashing at breakneck speed.

Ned was in constant pain, his stomach was always in a knot, and as he sat at his desk in his coat and tie, he clutched his midsection and threw up in the garbage pail by his desk.

Recalls Ned, "You have to realize: This was not like Intel going from 40 to 20. At least then, you still have the stock. My guys were on margin—their stocks went to zero and they still owed ten thousand dollars. You try telling a client whose stock has gone to zero that he still owes ten thousand bucks."

Ned's daily goal now is to make at least 200 calls to small business owners, doctors, and lawyers around the city. And he tries to meet that goal because, as he says, "Except for my mortgage, I'm behind in everything," his tone matter-of-fact. "I've liquidated every investment I've ever had; I've got $75,000 in credit card debt, and now I'm dipping into my 401(k). I've become a rags-to-riches-back-to-rags story. I started out selling videos in a shop on 42nd Street in my early twenties to make ends meet. I was always great at selling and I proved it all the way up the ladder at my new job as a broker. I fought tooth and nail for my rewards and then they were taken away. It's a slap in the face. It hurts that much more to have lived such a comfortable lifestyle and then retreat back to living like a recent college grad eating pizza." Self-defeating thoughts streamed through his mind such as, "I can't change this situation and this slump in my lifestyle won't improve anytime soon."

Back then, he says, he had nightmares every night. "I would get about three hours of sleep a night, and would wake up with eye twitches, neck twitches, and my skin would break out in a hot, itchy rash, that my doctor diagnosed as being eczema, a skin ailment exacerbated by stress." When morning would break, Ned was so depressed that, many times, he was tempted just to stay in bed. "I lay in bed thinking about how much I enjoyed the comfort of darkness in my room. I woke up next to my wife, yet I still felt alone and incompetent. When I made it into work, I had palpitations every day," he said. "But, I finally realized that I didn't hate myself; I hated my life."

Ned is no churn-and-burn boiler-room con looking to get rich quick. Back then, all his clients had his home number, and he fielded their late-night calls as they wept together over their wiped-out portfolios. He felt so guilty about one particular client who took a bath on one of his stocks that he still sends him a monthly check of $300 to help ease his financial burden.

Today, Ned continues to pay the rent and utility bills for his mother. "I used to feel so guilty, like this client's loss was totally my fault. It made me nauseated to think about it. I even starting going to church!" His wife is now on disability, and his expenses run to $15,000 a month. Since he's a commissioned broker, every month he has to start over to earn his monthly income. "Crazy things go through your head," he said. "Like trying to hurt yourself and go on disability. How about suicide? At its worst, I entertained the thought of ending my life. I fantasized about jumping off the Verazzano Bridge, and how I would enjoy one last rush before experiencing complete silence and peace. But that's a quitter's way. It took me a long time to get where I am. Doing that would make me a real loser."

Ned is not a bad man; he is a broken man, suffering, and he needs to be fixed. Chapter 3 illustrates how Bullish Thinking can help put Ned back on track with various strategies and comparative thinking.

What You Can Do Now

If you are experiencing pain like Ned or the Iceman, seek out someone you trust to talk to—your branch manager, a close friend, your spouse. If you choose your manager, it's important to develop an interpersonal relationship with him, to let that person know you are going through a difficult period. We have known advisors who have gone to branch managers and told them, "Listen, I'm going through divorce," or "I'm having trouble with my child," or simply, "I'm going through some personal problems at home." These are things the branch manager needs to know about, because if there is a direct correlation to decreased performance, then that will at least be an explanation for your behavior and you won't be anxious about your job or your performance—the problems are on the table.

Don't let misconceptions about appearing weak prevent you from talking to your manager. The biggest misconception on Wall Street is that you can't show emotion to your branch manager or your colleagues without being looked upon as pathetic. If you use emotion and direct communication strategically, you can get what you want and people will respect you for your honesty and being brave enough to show your vulnerability.

Furthermore, your manager or spouse will start to key in on supporting you and your business because you shared something with them. If you explain to your manager or spouse that you consider them to be on your team, and that your success depends on their continued support and guidance, they will feel good about themselves for having the opportunity to do something good for someone. In essence, your manager or spouse will feel validated for their job or role in your life. Deep down, everyone wants to feel this way.

As promised, the next chapter illustrates how Bullish Thinking helped Ned get back on the bull and how it can help you recognize bearish thoughts that hold you back. We'll discuss various strategies that can eliminate negative thinking before it becomes destructive to your emotional health, your job, and your personal life.

CHAPTER 3

Bullish Thinking

HOW IT HELPED NED GET BACK ON THE BULL AND STOPPED THE BEAR FROM GROWLING

Let's reexamine the concept of Bullish Thinking in brief: How we choose to see a negative event is directly linked to how we handle it from a physiological, performance-based, emotional standpoint. It will also affect how much we feel in control of ourselves within the context of work. *Bullish thoughts* are defined as rational, mostly positive, and based on personal and historical evidence.

Bearish thoughts are irrational predictions, expectations, and beliefs about ourselves, others, and our future. The helpful thing about this type of Bullish Thinking intervention is it teaches that *just one realistic positive thought has the power to wipe out an entire army of negative ones* that often hamper our moods and productivity at work. It uses familiar Wall Street language to minimize the negative stigma associated with receiving cognitive-behavioral therapy in business.

The Continuing Saga of Ned: Helping Him Get Back on the Bull!

Ned's story is a heartbreaking one, but not one without solutions, as we have illustrated in the previous chapter. As a solution for Ned, Bullish Thinking is a proactive, self-imposed intervention that empowers an advisor to feel as though he can take control over stressful or negative events. It transforms an individual from acting like a passive victim into a self-confident and determined player.

The number one ingredient that determines how effectively one handles a stressful or negative event is the thought process or self-statements that immediately (and we mean within seconds) follow the event (see Figure 3.1).

Now let's analyze some of Ned's alarming reactions to a protracted downturn in the market and to the decrease in his standard of living. (See Figure 3.2.) Specifically, he responded with particularly negative and irrational self-statements such as:

- "These people don't want to hear from me, and I sound so stupid to the other advisors who can hear my pitch."
- "I am not a good provider anymore, I'm inadequate, and incompetent as a husband and as an advisor."
- "I can't change this situation and this slump in my lifestyle won't improve anytime soon."
- "I'm a terrible advisor because this stock went down. I had no idea the stock would drop so much. I feel so guilty, like the client's loss was totally my fault."

Let's use some Bullish Thinking strategies to help Ned attack and challenge these *bearish* irrational, self-defeating, and catastrophic thoughts that streamed through his mind throughout the course of this downturn in his performance and lifestyle. Throughout a typical coaching session, Ned would examine each reactionary bearish thought and the consequences (bullish and bearish) that it created for his physical health, emotional intensity, performance at work, and sense of job control. He would be supplied with a "Bullish Thinking" monitoring log (illustrated later in the chapter) to aid him in learning this new way of thinking.

Bearish Thought Number 1: *"These people don't want to hear from me and I sound so stupid to the other advisors who can hear my pitch."*

This first bearish thought is a very common one for an advisor or broker dealing with constant rejection while making cold calls to prospective investors. He tends to personalize the rejection and may even feel more like a smarmy salesman after a while or an annoyance to the individual he is calling. Examining this statement, it is important to point out that Ned used a sharply defined type of word, *don't*,

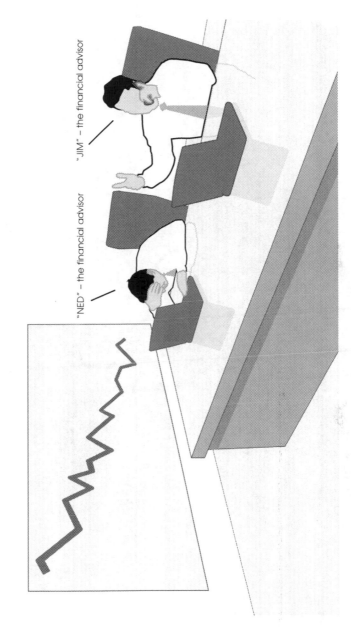

"NED" – the financial advisor

"JIM" – the financial advisor

Figure 3.1   Ned and Jim's Immediate Thought Processes

29

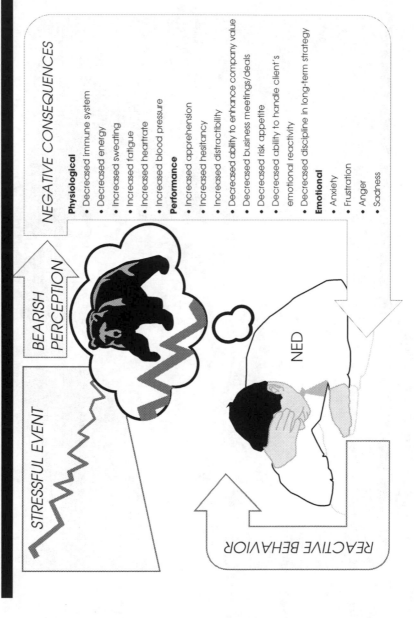

Figure 3.2 Analysis of Ned's Reaction

which, if left unchallenged, could bring him down even further in his mood and productivity. A sharply defined type of word or statement is defined as a cognitive error, because it leaves an individual no room in his thinking for fuzziness. To be more specific, such a thought pattern would see the sky as being either only sunny or dark and dismal. Ambiguity is frightening for an individual who adopts this style of thinking. For an individual using this mindset, there is no chance of seeing the sky as being partly cloudy. Every event is predicted to have a definite or precise outcome, which may lead to frustration if this prediction is violated by reality. Many Type A personalities or perfectionists experience this rigid type of thinking.

Bearish Thought Number 2: *"I am not a good provider anymore, I'm inadequate, and incompetent as a husband and as an advisor."*

This thought process is also very common for any individual who has tasted the fruits of success for a while and then later faces the harsh reality that he can't maintain the same caliber of lifestyle that he once enjoyed because of a decrease in pay. Ned's identity as an advisor and as a husband is locked into his monetary worth and, consequently, he feels worthless in both roles. The external and superficial toys that he once had access to are no longer available for him to fall back on. He's left with nothing but his negativistic and self-defeating thoughts. The key absolute terms that he must identify and later challenge in this bearish self-statement are, *not, anymore,* and *incompetent.* Together they lead to negative consequences for Ned.

Bearish Thought Number 3: *"I can't change this situation and this slump in my lifestyle won't improve anytime soon."*

Here Ned shows evidence of feeling powerless, victimized, and out of control in preventing his current stressor. The best way to describe this is to imagine someone trying desperately to run through quicksand and realizes that all efforts to move forward will be futile. He also is pessimistic that his situation will ever change. He uses bearish absolute terms such as *can't, won't,* and *anytime.* If he doesn't explore alternative and more adaptive ways of defining his slump, he will lie down and wilt during a time when he needs all the energy and confidence that he can muster.

Bearish Thought Number 4: *"I'm a horrible person because his portfolio took a major loss due to falling stocks. I feel so guilty, like this client's loss was totally my fault."*

Once again, this statement exemplifies Ned's propensity to personalize the negative events that occur at work, yet are really beyond his control. Many advisors feel personally responsible for their client's financial losses, and Ned felt so guilty that he even continued to pay back a client years after the fact! The key problematic element to his thinking is that he takes total responsibility for the stock going south, and ignores the fact that his client shares in some of the risk that comes with doing business in the markets. The absolute term that he should be alerted to is *totally*. He will certainly need to challenge the rationale for this self-statement to improve his outcome.

What Are the Consequences?

The consequences of Ned's bearish self-statements can be universally broken down into four outcomes, which tend to be predictably bearish as well. Let's examine them:

1. *Physiological:* Ned developed eczema, heart palpitations, vomiting, skin rashes, muscle twitches, muscle and stomachaches.
2. *Emotion (1–10):* Ned experienced significantly high levels of anxiety at an intensity level of 9 or 10. He also experienced depression, frustration, guilt, helplessness, and sadness at an intensity level of 8.
3. *Performance:* At work, Ned's contact calls to prospective clients dropped by roughly 50 percent, thus reducing his assets under management. He became socially isolated, withdrawn, and less inclined to attend company workshops or networking venues. He avoided calling clients back when their stocks plummeted because he was feeling guilty and afraid of their reactions. He had trouble getting out of bed in the morning because he felt as though nothing would ever change the outcome of his slump. At home, his relationship with his wife deteriorated and communication with her lagged. He retired to his den to drink alcohol at the end of his day and he became very short-tempered with her for any mistakes that she would make.

4. *Sense of Control (1–10):* The mere fact that Ned even contemplated suicide is an indication of how little control he felt in his life and at work. He sought alcohol as a means of escaping his feeling of powerlessness. He believed that he had no control over the outcome of the future and thus, he struggled to get out of bed in the morning. His bearish statement rendered him feeling vulnerable and incompetent with a sense of control that ranged from a low score of 1 to 3.

His colleague Jim's bullish reaction depicts a very different picture (see Figure 3.3).

Ned Uses Bullish Thoughts

Now that Ned is able to identify his irrational, absolute, and bearish first thought and the negative outcomes and consequences of thinking that way, he will try to manipulate these outcomes by challenging each self-statement with more bullish, rational, and healthy alternative ones. He will look to exploit the *absolute* words included in each statement by invalidating them with tangible evidence from his career or life.

> Bullish Thought Number 1a: *"I need to keep calling these clients because even if I succeed only once out of every 20 calls, by getting someone interested I have been productive."*
>
> Bullish Thought Number 1b: *"These prospects have no idea what value I am trying to offer them, and I know that people will never turn down hearing about something that has the potential to make them wealthy. Once I get them on the phone, I will prove my value to them."*
>
> Bullish Thought Number 1c: *"These calls are a necessary part of the job and no one else in my office really cares about how I sound on my calls. The guys who laugh at me when I'm on the phone are just trying to feel better about their own insecurities; I have to keep plugging away so my numbers will be superior to theirs this month."*

Instead of personalizing the rejection, he could have reframed the situation in a positive light and focused on the law of averages by thinking of Bullish Thought Number 1. As everyone in sales knows, this is lesson number one of prospecting. It's one of the hardest tasks to pick up when you are depressed. Ned accepted that it would be hard; he remembered a time when he had a broken arm and tried to

PERCEPTION IS EVERYTHING

STRESSFUL EVENT

BULLISH PERCEPTION

POSITIVE CONSEQUENCES

Physiological
- Increased immune system
- Increased energy
- Decreased sweating
- Decreased fatigue
- Decreased heartrate
- Decreased blood pressure

Performance
- Increased focus
- Increased ability to manage client's concerns
- Decreased apprehension
- Decreased hesitancy
- Increased ability to enhance company value
- Increased business meetings/deals
- Increased risk appetite
- Increased discipline in long-term strategy

Emotional
- Positive mood
- Confidence
- Stable mood
- Contentment

JIM

PROACTIVE BEHAVIOR

Figure 3.3   Analysis of Jim's Reaction

cut his lawn. It was hard, and cold-calling when he felt bad was even more difficult.

Bullish Thought Number 2a: *"I can still provide my wife with love, affection, communication, and stability, if we ride out this downturn together. I can prove myself to be a successful provider by overcoming this drought. Our marriage has made it through tougher times. This will make us stronger. Other advisors have gone through this before and no one thought less of them. This job is tough. Everyone hits rough patches. This event will make it more apparent to her that we are a team."*

Bullish Thought Number 2b: *"Despite the rough market downturn, I am still capturing more accounts than most of my colleagues."*

Bullish Thought Number 2c: *"I have always proved to my clients (for example, the Cohen account in 2002) that I was competent over time. They will understand that this is a temporary setback and that I have a clean and winning record as an advisor."*

Bearish Thought Number 2 is filled with absolute words like *not, anymore, inadequate,* and *incompetent,* which can all be easily challenged through personal historical events or successes that Ned experienced. Ned can create some empowering statements to disprove his counterproductive initial thoughts like about his marriage. To reframe his beliefs that he is incompetent and inadequate as an advisor, he needs to come up with just one real-life example to nullify his bearish thoughts. Or he could focus on the quality of the client-centered service that he has supplied his accounts with over time to reassure himself about their loyalty and willingness to make referrals when business is slow.

Bullish Thought Number 3a: *"There have been other slumps before, like in August 1996 and again in 2001, when I was able to make some great decisions on stocks for my clients, and then my referral list doubled."*

Bullish Thought Number 3b: *"All of my bad streaks have ended within three months and I have some money to remain afloat until then."*

Bullish Thought Number 3c: *"Just as I did in August 1996 and 2001, I will make enough money to reinvest in my career and quality of life."*

Bearish Thought Number 3 is based on another recurrent bearish belief that represents the hopelessness that comes along with a long protracted slump in performance. Ned can focus on the absolute words like *can't, won't,* and *anytime* to challenge them with counter-evidence. He will maintain his tenacity and persistence at work by recalling the above Bullish Thinking statement.

Bullish Thought Number 4: *"The client shares in the responsibility of the trade that I made on his behalf. I explained the risks and rewards of this type of stock and I could not have put the trade through without his permission. This is a shared loss and is the cost of doing business for everyone who takes a chance in the market."*

As evidenced by Bearish Thought Number 4, Ned apparently hates living with the burden of guilt every day. He sits with his losses much longer than he does his successes. His best bet is to understand that he is using an absolute word like *totally* when describing how much blame he deserved for his client's loss. He can overcome bearish outcomes if he says the above Bullish Thinking statement to himself.

How Will Ned's Quality of Life Improve?

The consequences or outcomes of Bullish Thinking about his work situation are generally far better than the ones we explored in relation to his bearish thoughts. Ned's work situation and quality of life can be drastically altered by challenging his initial negative, irrational thoughts, with more adaptive, positive, rational ones. If he practices manipulating his bearish thoughts into positive ones by using our worksheets, this new type of thinking can become habitual. Here we see his usually predictable improved outcomes:

1. *Physiological:* Ned will experience an increase in his resistance to eczema, skin rashes, and somatic pains. He will have a decrease in autonomic nervous system reactivity, thus reducing his rapid heartbeat, sweating, digestive problems, headaches, and muscle tension. He will have an increase in energy and a decrease in fatigue.

2. *Emotional (Level 1–10):* Ned may still be experiencing anxiety when faced with so much frequent rejection on a daily basis. However, some anxiety is always healthy. His level of anxiety is reduced to a score of 4 or 5, and his level of depression,

hopelessness, frustration, and sadness will become more manageable, plummeting down to a score of 4.

3. *Performance:* Ned's job performance will improve significantly just by virtue of continuing to make the necessary cold calls to prospective investors or follow-ups on referrals. He will increase his business fearlessly and won't shy away from risks. He will worry less about what his colleagues are thinking about him, and his conversations with prospects and referrals will be more confident and enthusiastic. Ned will be able to take a more proactive stance with his irate clients during a market downturn. He can alleviate their concerns and will be more active in addressing them on the phone. His belief that there is shared responsibility on every transaction will translate into fewer passive-avoidant behaviors when things aren't working out. As an overall benefit, he will bring in more assets under management (he is doing more fee-based business), be more outgoing, sociable, and determined in the face of negative events. Regarding his marriage, he will feel more capable of being an expressive, supportive, and communicative husband. He will be able to walk through the door at the end of the day and look his wife in the eye with confidence and happiness. He will be more emotionally available and less at risk for a divorce as well as substance abuse problems.

4. *Control (Level 1–10):* Ned will remain in the driver's seat at work because of his altered way of thinking and will likely report a score ranging from 8 to 10. He will do this while still acknowledging that he will never control the market and that his predictions and forecasts will, at times, be wrong. He will feel more capable of making tough decisions and will feel like he can proactively handle and change the outcomes of bad situations that are normal for the type of work that he does. He will feel like suicide was a sign of weakness rather than an answer or solution to his problems.

Ned's story was sad, but with counseling, coaching, and the use of Bullish Thinking strategies he was able to turn his life and his livelihood in a positive direction. He eliminated his stress, anxiety, and depression and continued his positive thinking. You may have known advisors like Ned or maybe you experienced similar challenges and emotional crises. As we continue to teach you the value of Bullish Thinking, we delve deeper into other issues that you may continue to identify with in some way.

Bullish Thinking Case in Point

Let's put Bullish Thinking into another context to illustrate other ways it is used in practice by two advisors, one with a negative attitude and one with a positive attitude. Sam and Bob are both 36-year-old top-producing financial advisors working in an established firm on Wall Street. They are both always at the top of their respective leaderboards during each monthly sales meeting. Both individuals specialize in the same type of investment process and strategy and both share the same types of high end clientele. One morning they arrive at work, listen to their voicemails, and receive similar hostile messages from their most important clients. The message indicated to each that they were "incompetent" and "pathetic" and that the client was going to "take my money elsewhere to get proper service."

It seemed that both Sam and Bob put their clients into an energy product that had not performed well because of events occurring in the Middle East. This type of scenario is extremely common for brokers and advisors and can create a feeling of hopelessness and powerlessness at work. The fascinating aspect of this all-too-familiar experience is how differently two individuals can perceive the same negative event and how their perception (bullish or bearish) can elicit predictable positive or negative outcomes that relate to the event.

Sam, like many other burned-out or stressed-out advisors, fell victim to a cycle of bearish thoughts on this gloomy morning. He received a message from his disgruntled client and slumped down into his chair, loosened his tie, and closed his eyes. Despite his great production numbers over the month, he felt beaten, tired, and incapable of picking up the phone to calm down his squeamish client. He had bearish thoughts streaming through his mind such as, "I am an embarrassment! He's right, I am incompetent. I am never going to get this client to trust me again. I can't call him! I don't have the energy to endure his insults. If I keep making these types of mistakes, I will lose all of my clients." In essence, he turned his anger at having lost control inward against himself. He wanted to go home and pull the covers over his head.

Although these thoughts might seem extreme and exaggerated, when lost in the heat of the moment, it's difficult to recognize just how irrational one's thoughts can get when colored by intense emotional states such as anxiety, worry, frustration, and anger. When paralyzed by fear and frustration, there are usually black and white or catastrophic thoughts at the root of it. Sam became a victim of his own thoughts and, during the rest of the afternoon, he let many of his accounts slip. He could not recover at this point and was unaware that he was sabotaging his relationship with his client and potentially damaging other client relationships as well. He would not make it to his important lunch meeting or complete his call list for that day. His branch manager received two complaints that day and he was written up for negligent business practices.

Bob listened to the same type of voicemail message on that ominous morning in his office. He faced the same character assassination and threat from his client for losing a large sum of money from the night before. However, Bob, took a deep breath, composed himself, researched the energy product by calling his wholesaler, researched the events in the Middle East that preceded the stock crash, and called the client.

Drilling Down

He manipulated the outcome of his day simply by applying Bullish Thinking to the stressful event he faced. Let's take a look at some of the bullish thoughts that streamed through his mind that morning:

- He viewed the energy product plummeting as part of the game, an acceptable mistake that was due to an unpredictable environmental circumstance, and as a challenge rather than a sign of incompetence.
- His attitude was that this was a temporary setback for him and his client and that he would encourage his client with new ideas and solutions and a reminder of his stellar performance and track record as his advisor over the previous three years.
- He challenged the bearish thoughts that Sam gave in to, with alternative and healthier ways of viewing a tough day, like saying to himself, "Energy is a risky sector to be playing with. I will reassure my client that this is par for the course and in following his wishes to grow his money, we had to take risks. We will reassess his risk tolerance for these types of products."

The result was that he called his client, learned that the client was only temporarily upset when he left the voicemail message and that he did, in fact, understand that this event was not related to Bob's ability. They decided to hold on to the product, hope for a comeback, and then they set up a meeting to talk in person the

BULLISH THINKING MONITORING LOG

WORK EVENTS Describe two situations, events, or interactions that lead to specific consequences.

1. Ned the Financial Advisor:

"A client gives you an ultimatum 'You have 2 strikes left' when you were a day late in organizing the transfer of his funds."

2. Jim the Financial Advisor:

"Facing a protracted market downturn. Many of my clients' profolios are hurting. A new client calls at 9:00 A.M. to tell me that I am incompetent because he has been losing money and his friend has done better with his investment."

PERCEPTION OF EVENT Stream of positive, rational thoughts, and/or self-statements

BULLISH THINKING	BEARISH THINKING	BULLISH THINKING	BEARISH THINKING
1a. "I'm going to take things one step at a time and write everything down. I will follow through with a To Do List' and maintain an organized and disciplined practice."	1a. "I'm too distracted. I screwed up and he *will* take his money elsewhere."	2a. "My strategy has been effective in the past. I will not second-guess my decisions or the money managers who work for me. We will stick to our long-term investing strategy. I will help my client understand the realities of investing and the long-term expectations that are required to minimize risk over time."	2a. "I *must be* doing something wrong with my strategy. My money managers are *obviously* not doing their job and I'm *going to lose* more soon."
1b. "I have a proven track record in this business and I developed a solid relationship with this client. He will leave his money with me to ensure positive returns down the road."	1b. "I'm going to lose all my clients if I keep making simple mistakes. This *will* be a domino effect. I will lose my solid reputation and my business."	2b. "I will stay disciplined and focused on my investment strategy. I will not be swayed by short-term market gyrations because the investor is bombarded by so much recent information. I will keep my clients grounded in reality and help them manage their reactions to short-term loss. I will make them money over the next 3 years."	2b. "I *should* revamp my strategy and replace my poorly performing money managers. If I don't act quickly, I *will* lose this new client as well as others who are nervous about this downturn in their investment."

CONSEQUENCES

BULLISH OUTCOMES	BEARISH OUTCOMES	BULLISH OUTCOMES	BEARISH OUTCOMES
Physiological **increased** – energy, healthy sleeping **decreased** – heart rate, blood pressure, sweating, headaches	Physiological **increased** – heart rate, blood pressure, sweating, headaches, muscle tension, insomnia, fatigue	Physiological **increased** – energy, healthy sleeping **decreased** – heart rate, blood pressure, sweating, headaches	Physiological **increased** – heart rate, blood pressure, sweating, headaches, muscle tension, insomnia, fatigue
Performance **increased** – confidence, discipline in strategy focus, retention of clients, clients centered and managing their reactivity	Performance **increased** – hesitancy, second-guessing distractibility, isolation, loss of clients **decreased** – discipline, client-centered services, ability to handle short-term losses & manage clients' emotions	Performance **increased** – confidence, discipline in strategy focus, retention of clients, clients centered and managing their reactivity	Performance **increased** – hesitancy, second-guessing distractibility, isolation, loss of clients **decreased** – discipline, client-centered services, ability to handle short-term losses & manage clients' emotions
Emotional low-①②③④⑤⑥⑦⑧⑨⑩-high frustration, worry, anger	Emotional low-①②③④⑤⑥⑦⑧⑨⑩-high anxiety, frustration, anger	Emotional low-①②③④⑤⑥⑦⑧⑨⑩-high frustration, worry, anger	Emotional low-①②③④⑤⑥⑦⑧⑨⑩-high anxiety, frustration, anger
Sense of Control low-①②③④⑤⑥⑦⑧⑨⑩-more	Sense of Control low-①②③④⑤⑥⑦⑧⑨⑩-more	Sense of Control low-①②③④⑤⑥⑦⑧⑨⑩-more	Sense of Control low-①②③④⑤⑥⑦⑧⑨⑩-more

Figure 3.4 Sample Monitoring Log

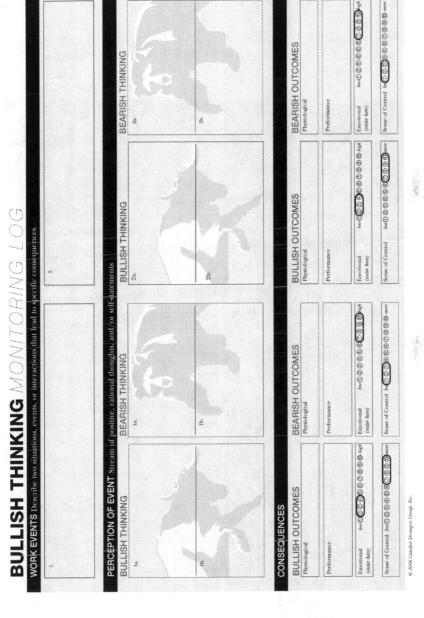

Figure 3.5   Blank Monitoring Log

following week. Bob took the bull by the horns, moved on to his next client, and a lunch meeting that was important for his business. He remained high on the leaderboard at his monthly sales meetings and is now looking to take on an extra administrative assistant to manage his relationships with accounts.

Take a look at the Bullish Thinking Monitoring Logs for various examples of positive and negative thinking, and their Bullish outcomes (Figures 3.4 and 3.5). We've included a blank one for you to complete.

STORY OF FEARFUL FRANK, THE TRADER

Frank was a 35-year-old trader stuck in an endless trading slump. At one time, he was a cocky, fun-loving character, but today he sat before me (Dr. Cass) with messed-up hair, a loosened tie, and shoes that were scuffed and very badly worn. Unfortunately, he was about as worn out from his job as his shoes that day. He talked about how difficult and what a humbling experience it was for him to trade in the volatile markets. He reminisced about flowing bottles of Dom Perignon and the lifestyle afforded him and his wife, who became unexpectedly rich in the late 1990s.

He complained that he had no desire to get out of bed in the morning to go to work because he truly felt he had no momentum to get through the sluggish markets. He noted that he was "trading scared" in a very uncertain marketplace, and he felt like he was a victim for having to give up his Lexus payments and new home in the leafy suburbs of Westchester County, New York. He explained that his stomach churned every time he had to make a tough decision about whether to buy, hold, or sell. Frank would often avoid putting a trade through and, instead, walk outside to smoke a cigarette or check his fantasy baseball team statistics. He would continue to have problems until he understood why he was so indecisive and fearful of taking risks—two behaviors that were not consistent with his trading style in the late 1990s.

For many advisors like Frank, that period was just a raging party. Many of them lived it up in their mid- to late twenties, and felt like they were at the top of their game and lifestyle in every way imaginable. Many boasted about their new properties out in the Hamptons, their late night partying with celebrities and cool new sound system. Trading was addictive and extremely reinforcing because of the success ratio that market makers and traders enjoyed. In a sense, you can compare the trading styles of some individuals in the late 1990s to that of a cocaine junkie constantly searching for his next high, disregarding all negative consequences of that behavior. It seemed like everyone on Wall Street was taking risks, and they felt invincible. One 26-year-old trader said, "Being so frequently successful and correct in my decisions about when to buy, sell, or hold, became addictive. It was like I had the Midas touch and everything I traded turned into gold, literally. I was hooked on the lifestyle of seeking highs and I could barely pull myself away from my trading desk to even take a bathroom break. With every success, I envisioned items that I would buy for my new condo in the city. I thought of the great parties I would have there and which ski resort in Aspen I would vacation at during the winter. It was a crazy time!"

Frank Starts Trading Scared

Frank's lifestyle changed drastically during the market bloodbath that negatively affected the lives of thousands of traders and investors in 2000–2001. He didn't have the lively and volatile markets to rush him out the door and into the office every morning. He felt incompetent and recalled losing money by the truckload on isolated days. He emphasized how embarrassing it was to be driving a Honda CRV to work at that point, and how it was a constant reminder of how much of a failure he was. As for his ability to complete trades, he felt completely dysfunctional and was unable to accept loss or take risks anymore. He was trading scared, and admitted to feeling like a "deer staring off into oncoming headlights." This trader, along with many others we have worked with, was burned very badly on some recent trades and felt great pressure from his family and fund manager to make more money.

Turning Fearful Frank into Fearless Frank

Frank was suffering from *behavioral paralysis*. When it came down to making a split-second decision of whether to buy, sell, or hold, he would obsess about his last bad trade and how accountable he would be if he was wrong again. I offered Frank three Golden Rules to help him in his business:

1. Don't Aim! Just Throw the Ball!

Fearful Frank was pressing too hard to be right on every trade, created by irrational fears, thoughts, and a nervous stomach, stemming from previous bad trades. He was not quick enough in his

(Continued)

decision making because he lost his risk appetite and belief that he was competent.

Dr. Cass: When I was 12 years old I pitched for a team in my local Little League. I was admittedly a wild southpaw but my coach thought I had potential. To this day, I can still hear him yelling at me between pitches to "Stop aiming the ball! Just throw the ball to the glove!"

I knew even then that this phrase would be meaningful to my life. Now I use these words with advisors as a way to get them to clear the noise in their heads before making a trade. Sometimes if you think too much or obsess over a past failure, you will think your way into a very bad decision that will cost you, like it cost Frank. If your research tells you which stance to take on a trade, follow it, be disciplined, and just throw the ball!

2. Go for the Batting Title, Not the Home Run Crown

Frank and many other traders lost a great deal of confidence in themselves by repeatedly failing on trades. My advice for these wounded individuals is based on a theory I developed called the Dave Kingman Theorem. Remember that Dave Kingman, one of baseball's great power hitters, had many more strikeouts than home runs. He was often embarrassed by crafty pitchers who fooled him on hanging curve balls that he was out in front of. Maybe it's time to look at yourself as a singles and doubles hitter who only swings for the fences when you are more certain of succeeding. Trying to be a home run hitter in today's market will make you experience a great many more strikeouts than home runs. In trading, too many failures or strikeouts can lead to fear, uncertainty, and paralysis, all of which prevent you from becoming a top-performing trader. Adapt your trading styles to the new markets and you will bring home the batting title, not the home run record. You will be happier and enjoy your profession a great deal more.

3. Think Bullish, Not Bearish

Bullish Thinking allows you to see the sun through the clouds. It is a technique that helped Frank and other traders get back to the top of their games, and to avoid trading scared. How bullish or bearish an individual perceives his past successes or failures will determine the outcome of future trades. When you notice that you are experiencing that churning feeling in your stomach while you are watching a stock price decline, that is the first signal to you that there are some bearish thoughts and negative emotions entering into your mind and body.

What you say to yourself at this point is critical for your success. Think bullish and understand that taking risks is part of the game and that if you stay true to your mental stop-loss position, you will at least live to see another day of trading.

Frank eventually traded in his Honda CRV and has progressed ever so slowly back to a respectable Audi. In trading, as in baseball, you are only as good as your last trade or at-bat; but in baseball some-one can watch a film of the player's successful moments. Appreciate and recall some of your triumphs and repeat to yourself three times when you get out of bed in the morning, "Today will be my day to 'just throw the ball.'"

"Irrational Exuberance"

As we all witnessed in 2000, the tech bubble burst along with the many grandiose hopes and dreams of many who had impulsively invested too much in overvalued tech stocks without diversifying. Advisors were inspired by the emotion on the Street before the bubble burst and clients were just as motivated to take risks with their money. They were all making emotional decisions and were neglecting the rational and fundamental truths about the stocks they were banking on.

In practice, we have noticed that many very successful CEOs, managers, and advisors have a quality that inspires and motivates others around them. Their energy and emotional intensity can become infectious. This is sometimes due to "irrational exuberance," or a state of mind that is driven by an intense positive emotion that is often characterized by a feeling of omnipotence, grandiosity, eupho-ria, impulsivity, and high-risk decision making.

The emotional highs can hamper one's decision making and lead the person to ignore very obvious negative consequences of his behavior. Emotion to an extreme can always lead to very serious prob-lems with your business, as it may propel you to behave in a careless and reckless manner. Even worse, too much positive emotion can create for you a blind spot, causing you to act in inappropriate or excessive ways without even being aware of it. Irrational exuberance caused the tech bubble and can impair your social and occupational functioning if left unchecked.

As we have seen with corporate scandals and deceptive practices throughout the industry, one can speculate that these individuals began to feel invincible and untouchable, both common side effects of developing irrational exuberance.

During times of irrational exuberance (as during the tech and real estate bubbles), we noticed that many transactional brokers were exhibiting symptoms that manifested as excessive phone calls to prospects (up to 600 per day), which generated numerous new clients. It is no coincidence that our markets did so well at a time when advisors began each call with high levels of confidence in the products that they were selling. Their energy and assurance sparked investors' interest and a desire to go against their better judgment to invest in highly overvalued stocks. The excessive phone contacts that were made during that time also explained the manic state of our markets in early 1999. Everyone was making money, excited about going with the herd mentality.

The law of averages would state that the more potential investors an advisor could call on a given day, the more new accounts she could obtain. Surprisingly, some advisors became depressed at this time, because their perfectionistic personalities led them to compare themselves to the top earners of each firm. If they were bringing in $200,000, they became angered that they weren't doing $300,000. They relentlessly called prospects to keep up with the top dogs of their firm. An advisor must compare her earnings to others around her and she cannot just walk away from her next trade. We've all heard the anecdote that the number one distinction between a transactional broker and a casino gambler appears to be that the gambler can walk away with his winnings for the day and enjoy it. It thus appears that the irrational exuberance of these transactional brokers contributed to driving the market share prices higher, but also in setting up the economy for an abrupt and debilitating market recession because of the irrational risks that were taken without forethought or following a solid hedging discipline.

Only one year later, after the dust had settled and the investors' wallets were drained, it became obvious that the advisors' confidence in their own abilities had taken a hit as well. The number of phone calls to investors dropped significantly per day in the transactional world of the brokerage industry, and investors became increasingly mistrustful. No longer did advisors go into work with the swagger they displayed one year earlier. Many reported having trouble getting out of bed in the morning because of intrusive thoughts such as, "What's the point?" In our interviews with advisors, they noted that it was very difficult to motivate themselves to make cold calls after the bell. Their belief system was that the investors "didn't want to be bothered" and the advisors became tired of repeated rejection over the phone. In essence, their negative thoughts and predictions about the outcomes for phone calls to prospective clients led them to display self-defeating behaviors; that is, not making calls to investors.

The lesson to learn from this is that there is a reciprocal relationship between advisors' moods and the highs and lows of our market. If advisors can find a happy medium between euphoria and clinical levels of depression, they would be healthier, as would our markets.

Use Bullish Thinking as Your Personal Check-and-Balance System

Bullish Thinking, as it is used to manage irrational thoughts that lead to depression and anxiety, can also be effectively used to maintain a mental check or checks and balances on an individual who starts to experience the early symptoms of euphoria, irrational exuberance, or increased sex drive, increased spending, risk taking, lack of sleep, and impulsivity. The key is to notice when your thoughts are becoming grandiose and when you start to ignore the consequences of your behavior. It is important for an individual to highlight on the monitoring log those words that may be perceived by others as being overly confident, grandiose, irrational, and brash. It is also important to explore all negative consequences for taking risks and the thoughts that you follow your own rules.

By challenging these irrationally exuberant thoughts with realistic outcomes and exploring the many permutations of outcomes, you can avoid major career and life pitfalls that could destroy your career, marriage, or perhaps put you in jail. Taking the time to think about some consequences when you are feeling too high on yourself is the check-and-balance you need to manage your emotions. The monitoring log will provide the chance to delay your action(s), allowing you to think before you leap.

In our next chapter, we explore some of the personality traits of advisors prone to developing the symptoms we discussed. We talk about rookies, veterans, million-dollar producers, and whether or not the type of advisor you are—commission, fee-based, or combo—affects the amount and type of stress you feel on the job.

CHAPTER 4

Mirror, Mirror on the Wall

IT'S ABOUT INTROSPECTION, AFTER ALL

Now that we've discussed the concept of Bullish Thinking and presented examples of Bearish thoughts and the accompanying strategies to use for positive thinking, you should have a pretty good idea of how these techniques can help you. The value of this type of strategic intervention is that it teaches you how just *one realistic appraisal or positive thought* can wipe out a multitude of negative ones. We also showed you how to maintain emotional discipline using Bullish Thinking strategies when faced with irrational exuberance. This is no simple feat, however. Once you have practiced these techniques over a two-week period, the ball is in your court to use them in your daily life! Remember the old saying, "You can lead a horse to water, but you can't make it drink." It takes practice and discipline, so be prepared to do the work.

There are certain personality types among advisors that are more prone to developing some of the emotional or troubling symptoms we discussed. In this chapter, we examine various categories (or types) of financial advisors—rookies, veterans, million-dollar producers—and whether the type of advisor you are—commission, fee-based, fee-only, or a combination of these—affects the amount and type of stress you feel on the job. We believe that each type faces different and various challenges, so it's important to understand some of the unique challenges of each practice. Most require *change* and *adaptation,* so we pay attention to the way our clients (the advisors) approach their challenges. You will see how the challenge of change can lead to powerful emotional reactions and resistance. In each case, it is important to see how you can adapt. No matter what type of income arrangement you work under, learning how to adapt to challenges in the job is critical to survival.

Look into your mirror; it's time to be introspective.

Who Are You?

Let's start with the traditional transaction broker, the professional who loves doing stock research at 7:30 A.M. every day, watching the market, trading, and whose clients enjoy calling and talking about stock ideas. These days, all wirehouses are promoting fee-based business and working with higher-net-worth clients. In essence, the traditional broker of today experiences stress every day from the manager, who insists that advisors in his office make the transition to a fee-based business before they are ready.

We spoke with a new client recently in his late forties who is strictly transactional and is very uncomfortable making a change in the way he does his business. He enjoys how he does it now—why should he change? Many commissioned brokers from 45 to 60 years of age have become very disillusioned and feel the industry has left them behind. They don't know how to keep up with the current shift to fee-based business. They are fearful of making the change and don't fully understand the income potential. They feel as though their firms are trying to push them out of their comfort zone—and they hate it!

If you are a transaction broker and out of your comfort zone, then you might feel like you are losing control. You may be a hard-charging Type A personality, for example, whose behaviors have been linked to a number of health problems, including cardiovascular disease and other stress-related conditions such as cancer, headaches, anxiety, burnout, and depression. A broker or advisor with this type of personality tends to be overly critical and demanding, even contemptuous of imperfection, and experiences a general feeling of discontent. In fact, research conducted by Dr. Cass ("Casualties of Wall Street: An Assessment of the Walking Wounded," catsg.com/casualties.asp, 2000), on financial advisors indicated that 96 percent of his sample reported that they were hypercritical of themselves for mistakes. The stress-induced behaviors exhibited by advisors with driving, aggressive personalities create a continuous presence of negative emotions that depletes energy reserves, wards off happiness, and disrupts personal equilibrium.

If you are this type of individual, and are forced to leave your comfort zone, you may be subjected to what we call *leakage.* Your negative thoughts prevail and you think to yourself, "Things will never change. I cannot do this." This is the absolute type of terminology we discussed in the previous chapter. "I can't do this. I'll never be able to make money in this new type of setup." "Clients won't understand." "I don't feel comfortable with separate accounts. I don't want to manage money." "I believe in myself, but I don't believe in the new products or solutions." "I just want to be left alone." "Why did they screw things up?"

Many traditional stock and bond brokers make a good living picking stocks, trading bonds, and keeping their clients informed of all the new opportunities and ideas. They are good at what they do, and the clients enjoy the relationships as they are. Today, many of these same traditional brokers look at the fee-based (or fee-only) system as "putting a client in a cruise control investment vehicle"; putting them into a group of funds or separate accounts and making the entire process automatic. They feel as though they are not adding strategic value anymore, and have to justify their fees. Their added value was in researching and picking stocks and knowing when to sell—*now* what is their value? What happened to personalized services?

If you want to transition away and do it slowly, you can turn it into a positive with this approach to your clients: "I will manage your money using third-party asset managers. You will have high-caliber portfolio management and I will supervise the process like a quarterback, but I will continue to call you with some appropriate stock choices and options, and I will attempt to make you extra money by picking good stocks because I'm a specialist." That's more of a black belt type of sales and service strategy. How you navigate through those waters using Bullish Thinking will make all the difference in the world to you. Instead of thinking, "I have to give up everything that I love doing to make the transition," use your transactional knowledge and your ability to pick stocks to your advantage. Then continue to learn about asset management or the investment management consulting process from a successful fee-based colleague. Or join a team of wealth management members and add your own area of expertise to the team. Remember, a team is only as good as its members. There are positive ways of thinking about your situation to avoid major stressors down the road.

Rather than a negative, bearish thought: "I'm going to quit because I hate where the business has gone," refrain from verbalizing those self-fulfilling prophecies. This type of thinking paints you into a corner. It will promote negative outcomes for you and create a behavioral trap. Make an impact on the outcome of a problem and try adopting a bullish way of thinking. Evaluate the situation and realize that those thoughts are too extreme. There is always room for fuzziness. "Maybe it *is* time for me to team up with another advisor who already has his fee-based practice up and running. Maybe I *will* make more money that way. Maybe I *can* have a dialogue with my clients and tell them I'm joining a team, but that I'm still going to specialize in doing the transactional business if they want. There really are positive aspects and value-added services offered through the various products and solutions at the firm; for example, asset management."

The benefits for you are you get to "Know Your Customer" (remember Rule 405) better and you will have the opportunity to capture more assets, and learn whether they have other accounts away from your firm. Look at it as a great opportunity for both you and your client. "I'm going to become more client-focused, I'm going to know my clients better, I'm going to be the financial therapist (or financial coach) to my accounts now rather than just tell them what stocks they need to invest in." So, we just take the negatives and turn them into realistic positives with Bullish Thinking. The difference is critical. With Bearish Thinking, the outcomes will be withdrawal, anger, and loss of motivation. The bullish approach leads to openness, assertion, and hope.

You're Happy . . . *Now* What's the Problem?

Let's turn to another scenario: You are a veteran million-dollar producer, you've been in the business for 30 years, and you don't want to make your business any bigger. You are a success and don't want to take on any more work because it will cut into your family and social time. Is there any hope for you if your manager says, "The office is going fee-based. Period. We are having too many compliance problems and the firm wants really clean business, and we don't want you to do any more trading."? Well, we can't imagine this happening to a million-dollar producer when a manager will put that much on the line, and risk losing a great stockbroker. But it does happen. And it is an issue of control. You control the situation, and your own outcomes with regard to the choices you make.

Before making a final decision on what to do, and before you go off the deep end, why not try the suggestions mentioned in the previous paragraph? Remember, you don't have to remain at the firm; you could go independent or switch from a major firm to a regional. There are a number of firms that will allow you to continue your business *your* way; you just need to investigate. The key to Bullish Thinking here is to gather enough data points to include in your thought process so you can make the best career decision and feel comfortable with that decision.

You're Afraid . . . Who Isn't?

If you are a transaction-based broker and have decided you do want to transition over slowly, but now that you're starting to make that move, you've become paralyzed with fear—fear of the unknown. It's something new, and you're having a lot of anxiety over it. Are you afraid your clients won't want you to transition over and leave them behind? Maybe you are thinking you need to spend more time cultivating the new business and that you, in fact, might have to leave some of your old clients behind. What are your challenges, what might happen to you emotionally and physically if you continue down the path of fear?

Behavioral paralysis, burnout, anxiety, problem drinking, problems with abusing drugs, marital problems . . . all these things can occur. A traditional stockbroker (we'll call him Pete) we have worked with is having a very hard time with these types of decisions. He feels beaten down, worthless, and inept. His standard of living has been decreasing because he can't keep up. This is to be expected because he is thinking in a bearish manner. He is caught up in a vicious cycle of behavioral paralysis and is viewing the problem as one big gray cloud. He is staring into an abyss and feels like the solutions to his problems are too ambiguous to be solved.

If this sounds like you, and you are viewing normal setbacks as a sign of overwhelming problems, and you feel as if you have one huge weight on your back, then Bullish Thinking can help you change your life. Try this type of thinking instead: Sit back, close your eyes, and imagine that you have many small weights sitting on your shoulders and that you are able to throw them off one at a time. As each one disappears, your burden will become lighter and the big problem will seem less significant. This will be your new reality. A healthy one filled with solutions to smaller problems. By restructuring your thinking, you will see a visible difference in your attitude. Be prepared to seek new information. If you were climbing Mount Everest, you would want to speak to someone who had done it. Bullish thoughts, like "First step, I'm going to take a colleague who has a successful fee-based practice out to dinner. He's going to share with me everything he knows about transitioning."

So, education is one path to power; one less piece of the dark cloud. As you create new solutions, you break each piece of the darkness down, a crack of sunlight starts to peek through, and hope is elicited. Next step, "I'm going to start to structure my day. I'm going to do my research in the morning from 8:30 to 9:30, then I'll service my clients, and I'll make some referral calls. I will begin to network, and talk to clients about the value of fee-based business." Then, you will create a business plan and a mission and value statement, and add to that your business beliefs and what differentiates you from other advisors. Understand that during this process, your negative thinking may be hammering at you, trying to pull you back into the quicksand.

This kind of homework and exercise—taking little tasks one by one—chips away at that black cloud, and you eventually begin to see progress. The secret is in tackling the big projects one piece at a time. It is important to look at a problem as a collection of small rocks instead of as mountains. The old way of thinking will freeze you and action will not follow. Act now, as if this is your last day to live. The challenge is that so many advisors in this business are oriented toward immediate gratification, and are not willing to wait for solutions.

Rookies: Can You Stick Around for a Year?

New advisors are quite vulnerable, and they have their own unique stressors to deal with. Rigorous training programs, building a client base, coping with rejection, handling in-house competition, and various other stress-producing elements are just a few of the hurdles rookies must tackle. According to the CBM Group, a Manhattan-based consulting firm that has monitored the progress of thousands of rookie advisors for several years—both in the United States and Europe—they report in their latest study, "Roughly half of a new class [of rookies] will drop out in their first year." So, add in the anxiety of graduating and a rookie has a lot that will keep him awake at night.

If you are a rookie advisor, take heed of our mathematical formula: *Happiness equals reality divided by expectations.* The point is that many inexperienced advisors have a grandiosity that historically has translated into: "I'm going to make a million dollars by the time I'm thirty-five or forty." When your expectations about the speed with which you will become successful does not match up with reality on the job, it can set you up for debilitating levels of disappointment and frustration. It is always important to research all that can go wrong and impede the achievement of a stated goal. Never rule out that something will go wrong or that things won't take longer than you expect. If you do this type of due diligence and identify these possible confounds, you will be less likely to feel overwhelmed when reality throws you a curveball. This type of cautious optimism will also help you guard against the repercussions of irrational exuberance.

Since the tech bubble burst, there has been a more conservative mindset among the younger set, but it's still a sexy profession to these rookies. But with the competition among firms recruiting producers with the larger books and those with the most assets under management, it has become more difficult to convince a firm that an inexperienced individual is worth the thousands of dollars in training, particularly if half are going to leave within the first year.

Rookies experience burnout rather quickly in this business because they pay their dues right out of the gate. They will make a lot less money than they initially thought they would, especially for the amount of time and energy that will go into the learning curve. Most of the time, their expectations are unrealistic. Reality, for many on Wall Street, comes crashing at their feet with a loud thud.

They need to adjust their perceptions about their job and their overall expectations according to the reality of where they're going, and hopefully link up with more seasoned advisors who can help them along and keep them motivated. If you're a lone rookie broker or advisor without any support system, you're really at the bottom of the totem pole these days. Tap into your available resources and learn from the best minds in the office.

Rookies Can Do a 180-Degree Turn

Jeremy was a rookie advisor who was referred to our program because of a six-month slippage in his overall production. He was initially touted as the rookie to watch in his branch and he had a variety of suitors (teams) that wanted to eventually snatch him up and include him within the scope of their businesses.

He was a 31-year-old MBA from an Ivy League school and was well liked by the other advisors. He was sharp, quick-witted, and hungry. Jeremy had high expectations, however, for his first full year at his prestigious firm. He was told in training that the sky was the limit for making salaries high in the six figures within the first three years of working as an advisor. He was eager to get going on building his solo business and to capture assets under management. At that point, the market was not cooperating, and clients were not as eager as he predicted to put their faith in his products and invest with him. He believed that he was a great advisor and he felt that his lack of production was like a slap in the face.

His symptoms began at the six-month point and were manifested as insomnia, muscle tension, fatigue, and rather severe levels of anxiety about his performance. He began to lose his stride around the office and he began to show up for work later than usual. He began smoking marijuana on a nightly basis and broke up with his long-time girlfriend. He was stressed to the max, not because he was not a good advisor or because he wasn't able to bring in business at all. He was failing because he was not meeting up to his overly ambitious and farfetched expectations for where his business would be after only six months in the business. He was his own worst enemy. His bearish thoughts were crippling him.

Those bearish thoughts included statements like, "If it hasn't happened for me yet, it never will." "I obviously am not as good as I thought I was or I would be managing more assets under management by now. All that effort and nothing to show for it!" "None of the successful teams are going to want me because I have proven to be inept at building a business for myself."

Notice how absolute his self-statements were (including all-or-nothing, overgeneralized, thinking with negative predictions), and think about how impossible it would be to be motivated with those types of thoughts streaming through your brain. These bearish thoughts and expectations of his future will continue to cripple him and his business unless he shifts gears and adjusts his perspective.

To alter the outcome of Jeremy's experience, we asked him to entertain a new way of thinking: Use Bullish Thinking with a longer-term perspective. He was caught up in the moment with an over-whelming thirst for a quick fix. He needed to adjust his expectations of how long it would take to be successful in his fee-based business. We asked him to explore the evidence that was available to him. He spoke with his branch manager about how long some of the other advisors took to blossom. He was shocked to find out that he was doing as well as some of the other big dogs in his office when they were just six months in.

His new and more empowering thoughts were written down on one of our monitoring logs where he was able to see how, by changing his thoughts to bullish rather than bearish ones, he could create a positive outcome of his mood, sense of control, physical health, and performance. He scrolled down statements like:

- "I'm still very young and have a lot to learn from my colleagues. It will get easier over time."
- "I will take Joe out for lunch next week and ask him about his benchmarks and milestones in his career so I can be more informed in managing my own expectations."
- "I was always successful and highly regarded by my manager; he will help me get through this rough period."
- "Everyone has started out this way; better for me now than when I'm forty."

In essence, Jeremy learned to think differently about his situation and survived the rookie jinx. Eventually, he was asked to join the branch's third-largest-producing team midway through his second year as an advisor. He could have saved himself a great deal of stress, anxiety, and a relationship had he sized up his early setback in a more realistic and healthful way.

Are Wealth Managers Immune from Stress?

Do high-level advisors and wealth managers who control upward of $200 million really need Bullish Thinking strategies? Those who already are greatly skilled and working with small to mid-sized institutional accounts, foundations and endowments, family offices, and the like . . . do they have bearish thoughts? They are successful, competent, respected, and emulated by their colleagues. What stress could they possibly have?

Living up to their fiduciary responsibilities is a major stressor. Capable and experienced, at this level of asset management they have the duty of ensuring that the institutional-caliber money managers they work with are staying within their style of management and are following the client's investment policy statement. They must constantly monitor the manager, and rebalance the asset allocation to stay in line with the client's goals. This duty is quite stressful in itself. Other responsibilities may include working with trust officers and other fiduciaries at the foundation and endowment level. Their wealthy family-type clients need estate and legacy planning, tax counseling, and business succession plans. Most times, these advisors will call in a specialist to consult with, or will be a part of a team that handles everything. All said, these are enormous tasks that can place severe mental burdens on an individual. The advisor may not have enough support for the workload; they need to do more client-centered service for their million-dollar clients, due diligence of money managers is eating away at their time; their travel schedule is hectic. How does stress manifest itself in these high-level advisors?

As it does in most everyone.

They will feel behavioral paralysis, fear, worry, anxiety, maybe even depression. It can manifest itself in all, or in any one of those ways. And at very high levels, too—up to a 10 on a scale of 1 to 10, 10 being the highest level. Performance-wise, these advisors may resort to such avoidance behaviors as putting off conducting performance reviews, rescheduling appointments with a high net worth prospect, or not willing to discuss why a recommended manager has diverted from his management style out of fear of losing a major institutional client. Losing control is a major disability for these successful advisors because if they feel they are losing control, even in a minor way, they lose their equilibrium.

Barry, a very hard-working and ethical wealth manager and investment management consultant, received his Chartered Financial Analyst (CFA) designation about five years ago. His business model includes working with high caliber, third-party institutional money managers. He feels more competent to approach and work with trustees of corporate plans and philanthropic foundations now.

His consulting process has six steps: Meets with client and determines risk tolerance and financial goals; he creates an investment policy statement that will guide the money manager; then determine the asset allocation; due diligence is done on the money manager and then chosen; the manager's performance is evaluated and monitored; and on an annual or more frequent basis, Barry meets with the client for portfolio review and makes any changes to the asset allocation or money managers at this time.

He has more than $700 million under management and works with a small number of highly visible international clients. To Barry's astonishment, he is making more money than he ever thought possible, but he is constantly worried that his major clients are going to leave him because of issues with the outside managers. His wife complains that he doesn't spend enough time with the family, and he even took a vacation to Paris to spend the time with a large family foundation—without his wife. He began to have chest pains and started taking an antidepressant medication prescribed by his doctor.

Is Barry headed for disaster?

There are no guarantees, but, in our experience, high-level advisors like Barry become depressed when they cannot enjoy the fruits of their labor. He was even avoiding his wife for fear that she would notice something was wrong with him. He was working longer hours on top of an already long day in an attempt to find an antidote for his panic. For Barry, his chest pains were likely a direct effect of his anxiety about keeping his institutional clients and managing their concerns about certain money managers who were practicing style drift and going against his clients' investment guidelines. He feared he wouldn't live up to his fiduciary responsibilities with the foundations and endowments, and that he wouldn't be able to help them with their ERISA compliance and the Uniform Prudent Investor Act (UPIA) regulations.

Barry's business is basically very solid, but there are certain things that are beyond his control, for example, the lead portfolio manager wants to retire but the next-in-line manager's performance is less than stellar. But, worry about the future can hammer on an individual if he doesn't remain vigilant of self-defeating thinking styles. What starts out as anxiety, worry, and panic about the future, can lead to burnout and depression if left untreated.

Barry would benefit from Bullish Thinking because it was his bearish self-defeating thoughts that were negatively affecting his marriage, mood, and physical health. His bearish thoughts were statements like, "If the lead portfolio manager hadn't retired, my client's investment performance would have been on track." "I really don't understand some of the new state regulations and I don't have time to do my homework, so I am going to look foolish in my meeting tomorrow." "My favorite money management firm is drifting away from their conservative approach and are investing in aggressive growth stocks and I may have to terminate their services; I don't know how to explain to my clients that I have made a mistake in choosing this manager." All of these thoughts were a direct result of his inability to sit with uncertainty. In this business, you better be able to manage it!

Barry can salvage his quality of life and probably his marriage if he shifts gears and begins to adopt the principles of Bullish Thinking. He could improve his mood, physical health, sense of control, and his client-centered services, all by challenging the negative thoughts that tried to paralyze him. He reformatted his thoughts into a healthier and more positive direction by penning statements like, "I will get through the rough periods as I have done before." "I have to focus on my institutional clients and manage their expectations before a change is made to the money managers." "I have to prepare everyone for the changes that may occur with third-party management." "I have loyal clients that I have managed assets for in the past. They are not concerned about short-term market drops because they are long-term investors." "Client turnover is part of the business and I need to factor that into my business model." "I will bolster my business by getting to know my clients better and instilling trust that I am adding value and that I am monitoring their portfolios." "Being proactive with my clients by adjusting their expectations about portfolio performance can save me later."

In our next chapter, we discuss the personalities of a group of allied professionals you frequently interact with at the office, what their own challenges are, and how you can work more effectively with them. We call it the Plight of the Wholesaler.

CHAPTER 5

Plight of the Wholesaler

HEROES OR VILLAINS?

Wholesalers, external sales consultants, regional vice presidents—the titles of these hard-working professionals are always changing. Much like the advisors they visit at brokerage firms, for example, financial advisors, financial planners, stockbrokers, traders, financial consultants, investment management consultants, wealth managers—some of these designations are enigmatic. But the *personalities, types, attitudes, and behaviors* of all these various titled individuals are even more mysterious. But if you want to build and strengthen your relationships with each other, it's vital to know each other's character traits and distinctiveness. Then you will know how to react or *not* react, respond, reiterate, or clarify. It's just as important (maybe more so) to be able to read people, so you don't intentionally push hot buttons or miscommunicate.

Do you want to know who you are *really* doing business with? *As a wholesaler,* do you dread going into your territory of 30 offices and seeing the same faces rolling their eyes before your presentation? Are the same big producers unpleasant or unfriendly to you? Conversely, do you find that your visits are met with enthusiasm by advisors who are glad to see you, and engage you in meaningful, business-building discussions after your presentation?

As an advisor, after the wholesaler's product presentation about the new socially responsible fund, were you turned off, or silently hoping she would leave soon? Or did you have a good exchange of ideas and investment solutions, and a resultant mutual respect that left you feeling positive about the meeting? Were you impressed with the creativity of the value-added service that was offered to your branch, or embarrassed for the wholesaler?

These experiences among industry professionals are everyday occurrences in our business. If the outcome of the visit was unpleasant and either party (wholesaler, manager, or advisor) was left feeling let down or exasperated, the entire event was unproductive and unrewarding for everyone. Let's try to make these occasions richer and more successful for you. Please read on.

Can't We All Just Get Along?

This chapter focuses on the approximately 9,000 sales professionals who many still refer to as *wholesalers*. They are also considered to be among the industry's unsung heroes. This chapter is also aimed at the branch managers and advisors who work, and have relationships, with them. So, to be of significant help, we believe it's important to address the demographic groups that work *with* and *for* one another, too. For example, wholesalers of mutual fund companies, independent money managers, and other third party providers or sponsors are the specific groups we want to reach. Branch managers, regional managers, traders, advisors—everyone needs to be singing from the same hymnal.

Members of the various demographic groups in this business eventually get to work with one another on some level—either directly or indirectly—and, hopefully, like beautifully crafted and well-oiled gears, they will work for mutual benefit, and for the ultimate goal of serving the investor. Or at least, that's how it's supposed to work. So, for purposes of this chapter, we begin by discussing the challenges of being a wholesaler, and that way the reader can take away a treasure trove of insight about this hardworking segment of our industry. We review the symbiotic, as well as the (at times) dysfunctional, relationships between wholesalers and advisors and how these groups can establish and maintain better relationships.

For advisors and managers: To attempt to understand what lies beneath, and to uncover what is behind the hearty handshake and the bigger-than-life smile; or the solemn face, the serious eyes, and the bark that comes out of nowhere during a presentation, we'll explain what we believe is going on. In doing so, whatever your professional title, designation, or job description, you will better understand the dynamics of your relationships with wholesalers.

For wholesalers: To help you understand your advisor audience better and to eventually navigate your way with ease through the maze of the five different personality types. (See Chapter 6.) We help you think of new and novel approaches for adding value to their businesses so they will enjoy your visits to their office. We also help you understand yourself a little better, too.

This Job Ain't So Easy

Industry studies show that good wholesaling jobs are harder to come by these days—more so than just a few short years ago. On average, this group is earning less, working harder, and their responsibilities have increased. The days of a wholesaler coming in, talking about performance, and making light chatter are mostly over. Now, it's all about value-added, training, mentoring, building business and, of course, the highlight is helping you buy their funds or asset management services. The old methods of selling are all but gone in many circles.

However, sell they must. And it must be subtle, entertaining, and educational. Often without any awareness of what new products are lurking around the corner from their higher-ups. They must find ways to excite the same audience with the same product year after year. It's a very tough business, especially with large communication gaps between them and the managers of the mutual fund they represent. Wholesalers have nightmares about how they will get in front of branch managers and their advisors on a quarterly basis without wearing out their welcome. They always need new hooks or strategies to stay visible at the largest producing branches.

Those in charge of the wholesaler groups at fund companies are saying that the old wholesaling model is broken and that some wholesalers are perplexed because all they really want to do is sell just as they were hired to do, but are frustrated because now they are being asked to do everything *but* sell. Some wholesalers feel as though they have become a commodity and are less able to influence advisors the way they used to.

They are now providing training on asset management strategies and training advisors on how to capture more assets from high net worth clients. Wholesalers are also helping advisors with time management, best practices, referrals, asset allocation, and even technology (all in the hopes that the advisor will look at the fund when it is appropriate for the client). The new wholesaler must understand the world economic picture, market trends, the pros and cons of new products, and how the entire investment process works.

On the advisor side, many complain that their meetings with some wholesalers are unpleasant and that they bring little or nothing to the bottom line, and they know nothing about building relationships. Some wholesalers complain that advisors are crybabies: "Help me solve my problems." "Help me get more wealth management clients." "Will you pay for my seminar?" "Get your money manager to speak at my client appreciation night."

Wholesalers say that some advisors don't want any value-added tools or help; they only want the hot dot. Wholesalers tell us that some advisors reinforce the old model by asking for another fund like the last one. Which fund or manager is performing best—that's all they want. They want a product pitch just like the good old days. They don't want the bells and whistles. Period.

For now, let's all agree that being a wholesaler and being a manager or advisor are stressful in their own unique ways. Individuals have their own personalities, their own attitudes, behaviors, and ways of showing stress. First, we need to respect those differences, then try to understand one another better. Let's begin by taking a look at the various personal challenges the professional wholesaler deals with on a daily basis.

Then, in the next chapter, we cover the five basic advisor personality types so that wholesalers can familiarize themselves with their audience, and advisors can also determine what type they themselves are.

Personal Challenges: The Sales Monkey on Your Back

So, let's talk about a day in the life of a wholesaler. Does anyone really appreciate what you do? Do the people you deal with understand the crushing stress you constantly live under? The driving force to compete with your colleagues, or how exhausted you are at the end of a long day on the road? We've listed a few of the challenges you face every day. Let's review them.

Remaining Upbeat and Positive about the Products You Offer

This is extremely difficult when your product is in a downward spiral; it's an obvious challenge and very stressful. Keeping up the optimism, managing the emotions of the advisors whose clients are currently in the fund will surely cause you a backlash. It's how you handle the backlash and whether you are adept at explaining the problems to the advisor(s) that will make all the difference in the world to your business. And to your stress level.

Solution: The Bullish Thinking wholesaler will be proactive and personally call their top advisors as soon as the performance numbers are in and be forthright and upfront about it. A simple explanation like, "We're down. You already understand the history of this fund, and we've gone through a four-month drought and have retained our gains over a full year and you can still expect to get our best management." It's one of the hardest things to do: calling with bad news. But advisors have to do it, too. So, you also need to help them understand the dynamics of what has transpired, give them confidence to speak to their clients just as honestly as you have. With an advance dialogue like this, you will have retained their respect and confidence. (It goes without saying that you certainly won't try to convince your advisor(s) of something that you don't truly believe in yourself.)

Keeping up the Pace

You have rigid schedules for organizing your day. Time management is a huge challenge. You must have breakfasts, lunches, dinners all nailed down; you are accountable for these meetings. You are constantly on the road; always talking; always eating; always drinking. You have no time to exercise, no time to stick to healthy meals. And what about time for your family, friends, and social life?

Solution: These are all things that are potentially dangerous to your emotional and physical health. It is important, when you are scheduling your lunch and dinner meetings, that you must schedule a time on your calendar for just yourself. Even if it's only for 30 minutes. Whether it is an early morning personal trainer or a long jog through Central Park on the weekends, it is important to maintain discipline for your physical health. With all of the great breakfasts, lunches, and dinners offered to you, it is important to monitor your calorie intake. Just because food and alcoholic beverages are available to you doesn't mean you have to indulge yourself in consuming them.

Bureaucracy and Communication Disconnect

Because of the many layers of management review, and regulatory and compliance hoops firms must jump through, it is sometimes difficult for you to receive adequate preparation and training for new products and other services as they come through the pipeline. Your firm may expect you to discuss, offer, and sell products without sufficient information, or at least before you are *comfortable* giving a presentation on them. Information gets hung up in the tight grip of hierarchy and red tape. Many wholesalers feel kept out of the corporate communication loop, and many don't know what is expected of them. They tear out of the office, hop on a plane, and then have to wing it, using a lot of fancy footwork during their presentations. All style, no substance. These wholesalers are actually perfectionists by nature, and can develop apathy for their job when they experience this disconnect from their products. They want to know what their product pipeline will offer in the future so that they can keep their assigned managers and branches excited and ready for upcoming products.

Solution: Go through the proper channels and proactively ask for conference calls with those in the know about future products. Explain to those above you that you are really energized and ready for another one of their fabulous investment vehicles. Politicking is important and taking meetings with higher-ups will give you the inside track. Don't passively accept the communication breakdown. Assert yourself and let everyone in the chain know what you need in order to be successful.

Competition

You are all competing for the same prizes every day. These days, there are hundreds of funds that will attempt to attract advisors' attention and will spare no expense to do it. You must be mentally prepared to fight for business and to expand your territory.

Solution: Keeping yourself upbeat and prepared for setbacks will give you the edge over your competitors. Using out-of-the-box presentations and value-added services will foster loyalty and repeat business. The key is to get yourself remembered and welcomed into a branch whenever you need to schedule a meeting. Do your homework about your advisors and remember their concerns. Keep a log of this important information to refer to before the meetings. They will be shocked at some of the things you remembered about them. This is how to be remembered and will differentiate you from the rest of the pack. Remember the issues on each branch manager's desk and try to solve them with value-added services. Some wholesalers sponsor best practice seminars, orchestrate key coaching and business coaches for top producers, and even organize etiquette classes for advisors.

Poor Product Performance

Yes, the relationship is important, and it's obvious you have to develop relationships with advisors and managers so they continue to welcome your visits, and benefit from your consistent service and your fund's or manager's performance. But, at the end of the day, if you don't have a product that is worth putting your people into that is solid and showing returns, and you have nothing valued-added that will differentiate you from the next guy, they're not going to call you again even if you are the friendliest person on Earth.

Solution: You are likely the type of person who needs to sell a product you believe in. Apathy can surface if your product is floundering and this will come across to your advisors. It is imperative to ramp up and foster stronger personal relationships with your advisors when your products are slumping. Give them confidence that your product will rally and keep them strong for their clients. When products are not peforming well, you must practice patience and even seek out coaching to manage your own disillusionment.

Feelings of Guilt

Sometimes a wholesaler might not feel positive about promoting a certain product, but will put a spin on it that *sounds* positive. He doesn't believe in his heart that the product is appropriate for the advisor's client. So, he is caught in the dilemma of trying to do his job, trying to understand the good points of the product, and trying to be client-centric, but not feeling very good about any of it. This evokes feelings of guilt, dissatisfaction, and creates stress.

Solution: Don't risk your reputation for the sale. This is a reputation business and under no circumstances should you push a product on an advisor that doesn't match his or her clients' needs. The sale will not compensate for the headaches you will have when the advisor calls you about his digruntled client who lost a ton of money or who has a low risk tolerance. Look for matches, not opportunities, and you will sleep peacefully every night.

Educating Advisors

The stress of having to understand all the nuances of all the funds in a fund family, combined with the stress of having to address and educate a room full of advisors (some not too willing participants) is enormous. Having to inform, entertain, and, at times, take the slings and arrows of discontent from the audience if funds are not performing as well as anticipated will make a wholesaler run for the pink Pepto.

Solution: This is where self-confidence can shine, and also where honesty and direct talk to advisors will serve you well. Honesty and bluntness is rewarded on Wall Street, so take on any objections with pride and confidence. In your presentation, try to prepare for all possible angles that could come back at you, both positive and negative, regarding product performance. Preparation is perceived by others as competence.

Value-Added Responsibilities

With the increased competition, and brokerage firms requesting that fund companies sing for their supper for the value-added services they can bring to the table, wholesalers experience another layer of stress. They must now prove that they can offer tangible benefits to the advisor. (Performance is still paramount, of course, but how do you differentiate your product against other exceptional products? Value-added service puts you back in the ballgame.) Tangible benefits are things like teaching mandated continuing education courses to the entire office. Or after a product presentation, leaving behind a voucher good for four CE credits. Help with transitioning to a fee-based practice, how to ask current clients for referrals, and how to organize and host a client appreciation night are some of the items among their offerings.

Solution: Find out more about what your audience needs for growth opportunity. Some of the best value-added services that we've encountered included wine tastings and an etiquette course for an entire branch. Value can come from almost anything, but how you package the service is the most important aspect.

Anger and Frustration

"I'm a salesman, I'm a product guy, I don't want to go in there and start training and coaching and mentoring and talking about how to develop your business." We've heard this a lot. These wholesalers feel they are not doing what they were hired to do, what they really enjoy doing. Why is this stressful? Because they are not happy. They become resentful and angry, then anxious or depressed. If this is like you, you can get caught in a downward spiral. Another real issue is the stress of trying to be happy (or appearing to be) in front of your audience 24/7 when you're really burned out on trying to be happy all the time. It's a vicious cycle.

Solution: The key is to be honest with yourself. Don't try to distract yourself from—or try to numb your feelings about—your job. It is very easy to think that alcohol or drugs are a quick-fix solution, or possibly even diving into more work. Doing either will only make the problem worse. Deal with the apathy or frustration. Try to sit back and write a list of all the positive aspects of what you are accomplishing with your job. What aspects of the job mesh with your personality or your strengths? Remember, the advisors that you meet will be able to read your dissatisfaction if you are burned out or apathetic about your product. No amount of acting can get you through that. Remain alert to burnout and take the warning signs seriously. Take a vacation and reflect on what you have accomplished to date as a wholesaler.

These are just a few of the challenges you face. Now that we are on the same page with each other, it might be a good time to try to understand your own personality a little better. Are you ready to be introspective?

Wholesaler Personality Types

Wholesalers tend to fall into one category, compared to advisors who can branch out into five different personality dimensions. Wholesalers tend to all be what we call *catalysts*. This individual has an ideas-and-actions-type of personality. On the outside, she is social and open to new thinking. She thrives on change and loves the action. Under high stress, she has but one flaw, one that can be fatal under the wrong circumstances. She is not detailed oriented, and the flaw is in not finishing the job she started. She is affected by emotion more than advisors are and has trouble hiding her dissatisfaction when her products are not selling well. She cannot hide behind a closed door or cubicle like an advisor for a few hours to hide her emotions. She is always on stage, needing to convince someone of the value of her products and of herself. This is a tremendous drain on her emotionally.

Of course personality is complex, and you may be a wholesaler who has a different mindset. Check out the advisor mindsets in the next chapter to see if any of the others fit you better.

Understanding the Personality Types of Advisors

By now, you realize how imperative it is to know with whom you are dealing. We believe it is the most important part of your job. It's no different from the advisor (your client) who needs to understand his prospective clients. It's the "Know Your Client" Rule 405. It applies to advisors knowing investors and wholesalers knowing their advisors (although it's not a required rule for you, it's smart to follow it). Understanding that every person has a different and unique personality and attitude and treating him as such leads you to better communication with that person.

In the next chapter we discuss the five advisor personality types. We believe you will find them fascinating and you will more than likely recognize many of these dimensions in the advisors you know.

If you are an advisor reading this, the next chapter is most important for you. Time to get out that mirror again.

CHAPTER 6

Do You Know Your Mindset?

WHY YOU ACT AND REACT THE WAY YOU DO

In Chapter 3, we described various Bullish Thinking strategies to help you address and cope with Bearish Thinking, regardless of your job description, title, and the circumstances contributing to your stress level at work. We all experience stress in varying ways, but we believe the positive solutions we offer can be custom-fit to your own challenges to help you increase productivity and decrease your self-defeating thought patterns. Advisors can be a quirky group of individuals and, anecdotally, share many common traits and qualities. In coaching sessions, they tend to handle feeling vulnerable early in their work with us by hanging on to their pride with all of their might. We see this occurring in casual conversation as well as in heated debates. Many times, they just don't want to appear to be wrong.

"I Don't Disagree with You"

When someone says, "I don't disagree with you" what does he mean? Does your stomach tighten when you hear those words? Most often, when someone repeats that phrase, it means that he is trying to prevent any chance of argument so he can speak his piece without interruption. If you find yourself doing this, think about the meaning behind the words, and whether you are sidestepping an issue. Are these words effectively communicating your desired meaning? If you used these words and the other person asked, "Well, then, does that

71

mean you *agree* with me?" And if you do, then you are using the words for another purpose, which is to avoid being wrong. Most advisors are uncomfortable with admitting in front of others that they are wrong, and would rather evade that task with this backhanded statement.

Sometimes, if you use this phrase, it only means that your thoughts are not well-formed enough yet to know whether you agree or disagree, and this pacifies the other person. One client of ours said that he leaves room for uncertainty in his conversations. He said, "I want to avoid giving the impression that I think I have it all figured out. I want to leave room for being wrong, for changing my mind, for the distinct possibility that the other person talking has knowledge or insight that I'm missing. I also try to remember that not everything is a debate. I used to switch into debate mode too readily, I think. I try to save debate for topics where I have a more considered position." Advisors take some time to give credit to others for being right, but once you have their respect, it can be very long lasting.

You need to pinpoint your unique mindset to understand yourself better, to learn why you act and react the way you do in stressful situations, and to put solutions into practice. Some people prefer to call this your unique personality. We like the term *mindset,* because as you approach your job, mindset is a combination of attitude and motivation. Mindset can shift while an individual's personality is likely to show the same characteristics across most—if not all—situations. Thus, one's personality is a description of consistent emotional, thought, and behavior patterns in a person regardless of the situation. At work, there may be a significant divide between mindset and personality because there are strong situational factors at play. To illustrate this further, a soldier may have a mindset of going for the kill on the battlefield, while at home, he is easygoing. *But his motivation in the field is to kill.* Unfortunately, if severely stressed, he may cross over and be very aggressive at home, too.

Before attending networking events, advisors must enter the room with the same mindset as the soldier going off to battle. Networking events like wine-tasting parties or golf outings may open advisors up to a variety of potential contacts or future meetings with prospects. These events are not all socially driven; there is new business at stake. Therefore, walking into an environment where there are potential clients requires an advisor to have a solid pre-game routine to get into the right mindset. An advisor who normally has any social fears or inhibitions must act and speak confidently and present himself as being polished in every way.

In working with advisors, we encourage them to develop a pregame routine that involves visual imagery and verbal motivational catalysts to get into the correct mindset. They need to block out irrational thoughts that may create fear or anxiety relating to making new contacts. They need to have a polished unique value proposition that will create interest in a conversation so they feel comfortable in any setting. The best one we've helped to engineer was with an advisor who decided on "I am a therapist for wealthy people's money!" This statement, said humorously, creates intrigue, and will encourage the prospects to ask you more about what you do. Furthermore, they will not forget that opening line, either!

But before we begin discussing mindsets and personalities, please keep in mind that as unique individuals, we find ourselves having some characteristics that may transcend or overlap two or more categories. Don't let this bother or confuse you. Just take a look at which profile or mindset contains a predominance of traits that you see in yourself. Go with the profile that seems to best capture your overall essence and style. It may be somewhat difficult to choose, because some of the traits in the various categories appear to be very much like you as well. The best way to decide which box to put yourself in is to think about how you might appear or come across to others; how others view you. Also, if you have many qualities associated with another category as well, it is sometimes useful to take the second mindset into account when understanding how you come across to others.

Now, the benefit of picking a category is really about not only understanding yourself better, but it also encourages you to seriously think about how others perceive you. By knowing yourself and which category you fit into, you can then determine how you can get along better with your colleagues, your branch manager, and your clients. You can better customize your client service to fit your client's personality by knowing what they want or how they want to be treated by you. This is the point of our first exercise: getting to know your own mindset, to better know yourself and others.

Let's get started describing the mindsets and the various ways that you approach your life, your family, your job, your clients, your manager, and your challenges. Your mindset dimensions emerge in a clear-cut way while you are under stress, so keep that in mind as you browse the checklist in Figure 6.1. The introspective process allows you to honestly review the traits in each column; then check off which of the attributes apply to you. The category with the most check marks points to your mindset.

After you finish your list, and you've had time to reflect on your findings, decide whether you agree or disagree with your review of yourself. If you are a little confused, take some more time to think about yourself. Try going over the list again to see whether your

THE CATALYST	THE VOICE OF REASON	THE DECISION-MAKER/PROBLEM-SOLVER
• Magnetic • Enthusiastic • Optimistic • Friendly • Warm • Superficial • Demonstrative • Political • Creative-abstract thinker • Distractible • Socially driven • Influencing • Trusting • Overtly emotional • Perceived as the "social butterfly" • Risk taker • "Out of the box" solutions • Eccentric behaviors and interests • Stimulation seeker • Self-promoter	• Patient • Predictable • Reliable • Steady • Relaxed • Modest • Nonconfrontational • Perceived as unemotional • Follows • Sticks to the rules • Avoids risks • Painful emotions are masked • Appears confident during crisis • Meticulous • Thoughtful decision making • Requires trust	• Ambitious • Forceful • Decisive • Strong-willed • Independent • Goal-oriented • Quick to anger • Impatient • Intimidating • Concrete facts and outcomes measures preferred • Perceived as arrogant • Blames others for mistakes • Unaware of self or others' emotions or skill deficits • Territorial • Demanding • Entitled • Calculated risk-taker

THE PERFECTIONIST/FACTS AND DETAILS	THE CONTRARIAN
• Dependent • Neat • Conservative • Perfectionist • Careful • Compliant with rules and regulations • Prefers facts and data to make decisions • Slow decision makers • Prefers isolation from others • Analytical thinker • Enjoys research • Sensitive to anxiety and worry • Risk averse • Introverted • Socially uncomfortable	• Frequently takes the opposing position • Blunt • Focused on meeting the bottom line • Prefers empirical data to qualitative • Enjoys attention and the spotlight • Nonconformist • Adversarial in nature • Enjoys conflict • Has only several close colleagues • Seen as quirky • Agnostic beliefs • Intellectual elitist • Socially withdrawn and isolated • May be seen as having an abrasive style • Demanding • Little tolerance of slower-thinking individuals

Figure 6.1   The Five Advisor Mindsets and Their Traits
Source: Copyright © 2007 by Catalyst Strategies Group, NYC.

perception of yourself changed at all. It's a good idea to show your list to a colleague, friend, or your spouse to determine whether any of them perceive you the same way that you perceive yourself. If the individual reviewing your list says, "That's nothing like you," then you might be feeling *one way* about yourself and the world might be seeing you *another way;* it might be a lack of insight on your part that makes the difference. Or, it may be that you have hidden an aspect of yourself from others.

Mind you, this is not necessarily a pathology, but rather an incompatibility indicating that you may be constantly at odds with your internal self versus your external self. This lack of synergy between your internal insight about yourself and how you perceive yourself to come across to others may set someone up for burnout if it is not addressed. This is something to think about if this occurs with you (and it may be difficult to face)—you may be forcing yourself into a job that is not really meant for you or that you are not really happy doing. It is worth thinking about.

Now, let's take a more in-depth look at the individual mindsets and how the traits manifest themselves.

Mindset: The Decision-Maker/Problem-Solver

You are a calculated risk taker. You focus solely on the bottom line, measured in results. You care only about the results and will base your success on those results. You are decisive, extremely competitive, and usually harbor a great deal of anger that comes out in bursts when you are frustrated (you have the highest propensity for taking it out on colleagues, assistants, and clients). You have a tendency to make decisions based on fewer data points than other mindsets require. You tend to have little patience, are quick to make decisions—typically, quicker than most; that's what makes you successful. You may have an extremely difficult time working with others who think slowly or act slowly. It drives you crazy. You tend to be perceived as being arrogant, but are not necessarily that way. You may tend to blame others for your mistakes.

Mindset: The Catalyst

If you are a Catalyst, you tend to create energy in the office and among clients. You are often an effective change agent. You have the tendency to be open to new experiences and take risks. You may often demonstrate eccentric behaviors and interests and may be capable of producing out-of-the-box solutions. Your preference for creative abstract thinking may cause problems for more conventional clients, and for your colleagues and manager.

Your conscientiousness is moderate as you respond to external pressure and may be quite motivated when you have an opportunity to influence others. Catalysts tend to be extroverts and can be viewed as dynamic, even magnetic, and are usually friendly and socially driven. Catalysts have a tendency to be overly agreeable. While you are enthusiastic and optimistic about your own ideas, you may sometimes appear as superficial and political. Also displaying a tendency toward being a social butterfly, you quickly retreat if you perceive that others may challenge or threaten you. When your expectations don't match up with reality, however, you are more at risk than any other mindset for experiencing behavioral paralysis. The inclination to be overly optimistic about your abilities can set you up for emotional upheaval if you experience a minor setback. Charlie Sheen's character, Bud Fox, in the movie, *Wall Street,* was a catalyst . . . aggressive and competitive, but he also was a dreamer.

Mindset: The Voice of Reason

As the Voice of Reason, you tend to be reliable, steady, and make thoughtful decisions. You may not get rattled easily, and will stick to the rules, so you rarely have compliance problems. You may be slow to offer trust, however, and it is only developed after careful consideration and you insist that others must prove over and again that they are trustworthy. In essence, the Voice of Reason has a great deal of the Catalyst and the Decision-Maker/Problem-Solver running through his veins. It is the happy medium between the other two mindsets.

Unfortunately, you tend to mask your emotions, you don't let people in easily, and you don't readily show them who you are. Others can be put off by you, and your colleagues will actually think you are not interested in them. This can be a big problem for you, especially when dealing with your manager.

You are inclined to be unusually conservative with clients' money because you are generally not a risk taker. You are not flashy and you don't like much social interaction or partying. You work by the book, you are respected, and are a very controlled individual. You are perceived as a polished individual who doesn't rock the boat. Clients tend to be as conservative as you are. Conflict with clients tends to rattle you more than it does for other mindsets. You will likely not communicate your dissatisfaction with a conflictual office situation and this leads to more problems for you later.

Mindset: The Contrarian

Contrarians have the inclination to go against trends, don't care about being tactful, and don't care what people think about them. If you are a Contrarian, you may come across as extremely arrogant and intellectually elitist. You probably are a complete renegade, many are atheists, and some people consider your behavior to be a bit bizarre or humorous.

You, like the Voice of Reason, tend not to be a sociable person and are particularly awkward in a social setting. You may treat others at work as if they are a means to an end, and this remains your work persona. You may be more emotional and sensitive in your personal life, but you may have a tendency to discount others' feelings in the business setting. Most times, you do not have the skills to look outside of yourself because you tend to be in your own world. Contrarians don't often take the time to think about what others are feeling or thinking. It's not that they don't care; they are just not aware. You are like the Lone Wolf and you say to yourself, "No one is going to tell me what to do. I'm doing my own thing, regardless of what anyone else is doing." You are rebellious.

You may tend to dress in a quirky fashion and are eccentric in your investment styles as well. You have the potential of being extremely successful, like many innovative entrepreneurs are. The Contrarians are rare birds. About 5 percent of the audiences we speak to claim to be Contrarians.

Mindset: The Perfectionist/Facts and Details

Individuals who are the Perfectionist/Facts and Details type would make great compliance officers. They tend to be analytical thinkers and will run their practice by the book. Most abhor taking risks and, thus, do not make very good entrepreneurs on their own. They are generally the type who will remain at a large brokerage firm and not attempt to go independent even if it meant making more money, having more control, and enjoying more freedom. If you are this type of advisor, you are a great analyst, perhaps a great financial planner.

Typically, you are orderly, neat, quiet, and perfectionistic. You will make sound research decisions, don't like risk, and are completely averse to it. You may require many data points before feeling comfortable in making a decision about a trade. Having a lot of internal anxiety, you can be driven by obsessional thoughts. You need things in order.

Some of the troublesome aspects of being a Perfectionist/Facts and Details person is that you tend not to think out of the box enough, are not as creative in your marketing methods, and almost never ask for referrals. Since you need to be in control of all things, you may be in a lot of trouble in a world that is filled with uncertainty, and especially in the markets. Conflicts with colleagues, managers, or clients can make you feel overwhelmed. You are inclined to avoid conflict at all costs and have trouble communicating your feelings in an assertive manner. As an introvert, you will likely repress anger or frustration with a colleague or client. This can later end up with you burning out. You entered this uncertain business because you love numbers. Math is comfortable and safe, whereas selling and servicing clients creates stress for you.

Do It for Your Clients

As you can see, the characteristics in the categories are for the most part unique to each individual, although as we mentioned at the beginning of the descriptions, some characteristics overlap, so be mindful of that, but analyze yourself on the basis of trait predominance.

This exercise is important because you must truly know yourself to present yourself in the most correct and appropriate manner to a prospect or client, but most important, so you can be the most client-centered service advisor you can be.

Can You Really Change or Adapt Your Mindset?

As stated previously, it is impossible to change your mindset to any significant degree, but *it is possible to change how you come across to others* in everyday life. It is crucial, however, to first know yourself and how others perceive you in a natural state. That is how the journey begins. We ask that you categorize yourself into one of the five mindsets to jumpstart this introspective process. After you truly admit to your personality's strengths and weaknesses, you can then effectively adapt your style or mindsets to each and every new client or colleague you come across. For example, an advisor who knows that he has a Perfectionist/Facts and Details mindset may have to overcome fears about dealing with a complex social networking event. He may hate small talk and express very little emotion in social settings. When faced with the challenge of a wine and cheese event, these individuals will have to act as if they are more extraverted and energetic than they really are. For them to do this, they must feel like they are going against the grain, by feeling the anxiety of remaining open to new people and the risks of rejection. In practice, we often assign advisors who have the Perfectionist/Facts and Details mindset to focus on adapting their behavioral habits for the sake of attracting new types of clients. For the most part, acting naturally, they will turn off or bore an energetic, extraverted power client. In this scenario, we encourage them to leave the event with at least 10 business cards and give out 10 of their own.

We also help these individuals create intriguing and structured opening lines to get a conversation started. Once they have the tools to work a room, their anxiety is reduced and prospective clients feel like this person is more approachable. Thus, the second step of this process is to gain a thorough understanding of the variety of client styles that you may come across in business.

As you will see in the next chapter, we offer 10 in-depth personality profiles of typical clients that you may currently work with or may work with in the future. We present some strategies such as using these investor profiles to segment your book of clients, which will help you learn how to best interact and service them for higher retention and higher referrals.

CHAPTER 7

The 10 Investor Styles

HOW TO INTERACT WITH THEM SUCCESSFULLY

Now that you've studied the various advisor mindsets described in the previous chapter, and have reviewed your own list of traits, you probably understand a little bit more about your own behaviors and attitudes. And, if you were bold enough, you showed your list to a colleague, your manager, a close friend, or a family member. Did you find that others perceive you differently from how you perceive yourself? Sometimes when that happens, we choose to ignore it and distract ourselves further by diving back into our busy work. But we hope you received meaningful feedback and were able to incorporate their comments into any behavioral changes you feel it is necessary to make.

By understanding your mindset, you can also better customize your client service to blend with your client's personality (which we discuss next) by knowing what they want or how they want to be treated by you. This was the key purpose of our exercise in the previous chapter: getting to know your own mindset to know yourself and others better, and to avoid or deal with stressful situations in a more positive manner.

Rationale for Understanding Investor Types and Profiles

Based on numerous conversations over the years with countless advisors and brokers, we have determined that there are about 10 different investor profiles, each having distinct character traits. We gave them titles that matched their unique traits so we could more easily identify them during our sessions with advisors.

We present these 10 investor profiles and describe each one in detail. We're sure you will recognize many of them as your clients. By going through this exercise of learning and understanding investor profiles, you should feel encouraged to ask your clients key questions about themselves to determine their type and to know how they feel about risk, reward, money, education, family, politics, philanthropy, society, the world, and so many other things, including *you,* their advisor.

If you are thinking, "But I already go through this exercise with my clients," you are probably right, but the battle is only half over. You have an initial questionnaire that you discuss with your clients. Many of the questions on the form will relate to risk tolerance, lifestyle, investments, goals, and such. This is your external blueprint to help them reach their goals (and some call it their Policy Statement). This document, however, does not really give you the inside information about their personality, their mindset, their attitudes, or behavior. And it doesn't really help you pinpoint *who* they are and *why* they think and behave the way they do. If you can understand the subtle nuances of their mindsets, then you have a better chance of retaining these clients for life. You can relate better, empathize, and connect on a higher level. This builds a layer of trust that ultimately cements the relationship and allows you to invest and manage their money with more confidence. You will capture more of their assets, get exceptional referrals from them, and build your business by leaps and bounds. Also, if you can identify which type of client you are presenting to on a first meeting, you can tailor your approach to be more appealing to that mindset. When it comes to meeting with a prospect for the first time, you often get just one chance to present yourself and your products in the best possible light just that one time. You must use the interview questions and your ability to generalize, based on the prospect's profession and phone manner to size him up.

Some may say that this looks like subtle manipulation; that is, telling the client what she wants to hear or mimicking that person so you can sell them something. Well, we don't subscribe to that line of thought. You *are,* in fact, selling *yourself,* and to do that in an honest and ethical way you need to find some common ground through the questioning process and demonstrate that you sincerely want to give your client the highest possible service and value. We can't deny that the foundation of this business was built on selling and servicing. The most successful advisors know how to do both, and do it in a way that is client-centered and not just to make a commission or a fee. Understanding your clients' needs, fears, and other personal aspects of their lives is not a manipulation to sell something or anything. It is a very real method of getting to the core of their personality so that what you *do* sell, recommend, and advise is a perfect fit and that the relationship benefits because of that.

We are psychologists and in many ways we think of ourselves as salesmen. Are you surprised? Most people would be appalled by the thought that a psychologist should be a salesperson, but think about it this way: If you need help or counseling, you have a choice between us and thousands of other psychologists. Why would you decide on us? It would be because we sold you on our competence, our skill, our experience, and our compassion. That doesn't mean we manipulated you, not at all. It means that we took the time to relate to you, to understand what your mindset is, and impressed you because of our ability to empathize with your complaints or symptoms. Because of our emphasis on a practical, scientifically based therapy, the advisors believed that we could help them.

Knowing how to read people is very important. Sometimes it is innate; sometimes it is a learned skill that helps you in business, in social circles, with friends, and with family. It really helps you understand how people want to be treated, in ways that make them feel comfortable and willing to trust in your abilities. When dealing with clients' money, these exercises are not a luxury, entertainment, or pop psychology; it's a necessity.

Characteristics of the 10 Investor Profiles

The following 10 investor profiles each display clear and separate personality traits. The tongue-in-cheek titles correspond with their traits so you can remember them more easily during the learning process. Do you recognize any of them as current clients?

1. *The Grand Inquisitor.* This type of client is usually very naïve, may be a first-time investor, and asks numerous questions. This is due to the great anxiety they face in new or unfamiliar situations. They need a lot of hand-holding and require

careful and in-depth clarification about all of the investment products, including the pros and cons of each. Since they are very risk averse, be careful about recommending large capital commitments too early in the relationship. This client will tend to call you frequently, asking more questions and looking for reassurance that he made the right decisions.

2. *Neurotic Ned.* An individual like Ned has an enormous amount of emotional baggage related to previous bad investments or bad experiences with unskilled advisors. Like the Grand Inquisitor, his underlying anxiety about investing is high and he is very risk averse, at least initially. Neurotic Ned will benefit from quick returns, albeit small, and he will then consider taking more risk. You might try working your way up with this type of client by making small, incremental investments early on in the relationship.

3. *The CEO type.* Be on your best behavior with this type of client. He has an explosive temper, expects competence, has no time for small talk or fakery, and will fire you in the blink of an eye if you are not accountable, responsive, and highly skilled. He is very results-oriented, so you must do thorough research on anything you recommend to him, as he will hold you to task on everything. He wants the top products and wants a proven track record before he invests. Highly competitive, he is also a risk taker, so you can discuss higher-level products and investment solutions with him such as hedge funds and private equity, if he is qualified. Keep in mind that he will invest his money with other advisors.

4. *The Miser.* This individual is a conservative investor and tends to horde money. He harbors serious issues of control, usually rooted in anxiety. He is not a flashy individual, is not impressed by those who are, and their own sense of fashion leaves much to be desired. The Miser is extremely anxious about loss, and is uptight about their investments. They have a strong need to feel in control of their accounts. They usually live far below their capabilities, and have issues with indulgence. Stereotypic interests and hobbies may include coin collecting and bird watching. This person may be the millionaire-next-door type because they are usually self-made individuals. Misers are skeptical, slow decision makers, and can be very loyal, long-time clients. They don't make decisions rashly.

5. *The Politician*. Easygoing and energetic, this individual is a dreamer and likes to think out of the box. This is good, because he is not afraid of risk. He enjoys flashy presentations with PowerPoints, charts, and visuals, but remember that he is averse to facts, figures, and details. As far as conversations go, he is the type that prefers the superficial chummy exchanges. He will be very impressed with your success and track record, especially if you have a large number of assets under management.

6. *The Micro-Manager.* The first thing to be aware of is that this client is a high risk for litigation. He is very obsessive, requires everything in writing (no handshakes for him), examines all documentation carefully, and enjoys the facts and figures of your presentations. His personality is conservative and he requires conservative investments; no flash or superficiality for him. This will turn him off immediately. He is a moderate risk taker.

7. *The Risk Taker/Thrill Seeker.* This is the kind of client you can really have fun with, if you are of like mindsets, because he would be very impressed with your style. He enjoys the rush of investing in volatile markets, thinks risk-taking is an adventure, and has a strong stomach for loss. If you provide a great presentation on risk versus reward, you will have a client ready to do business.

8. *Mr. and Mrs. "Look-at-Me."* These individuals are superficial, materialistic, and arrogant. They are your typical celebrity types, impressed with the assets you have under management and how successful you are or appear to be. They are interested only in top-name investments and products. They would be perfect for separately managed accounts and high-level products such as hedge funds and direct investment, such as oil and gas or equipment leasing programs. They don't want to be involved in the process and remain naïve about the world of investing. Like the CEO type, they usually have their assets with multiple advisors.

9. *The Flake.* You may want to reconsider this type of client. The Flake is usually a one-time investor, that is, "here today, gone tomorrow." He has an impulsive personality, loses paperwork, misses appointments or reschedules at the last minute, and does not return phone calls. If you really want to help this individual, you can try to impress upon him the importance of having consistency—not only in his life—but also in his

investment outlook. If you're lucky, he will appreciate the education and the advice. But don't count on it.

10. *Steady Mr. Goldfinger.* Even though he is slow to trust, this client will be loyal and attentive. You can build this trust by achieving small gains with certain products or investments. He will also benefit from facts and figures, and appreciates your explanation of them. In the beginning, he will show his conservative side, and then with investment success, he will develop a healthy appetite for risk. He is slow to get angry and he hides his emotional side, so be as tuned in to him as you can be. He expects you to be highly skilled, experienced, and polished.

How You Interact with Your Investors' Profiles

In this next section, we give you a brief overview of who you do and don't naturally work well with vis-à-vis the 10 investor types and how they match up to your own mindset. Then we give you the strategies for working with each one.

As a *Decision-Maker/Problem-Solver,* a Miser profile might be impressed with you, but you like to make quick decisions with little information needed and might be too quick to need an answer from a Miser and that might not work out well. The Misers tend to be impressed by Decision-Maker types like you, more so than anyone else. Other investors not working well with you are the Grand Inquisitor, Nervous Ned, Micro-Manager, and the Flake. On the other hand, you would enjoy working with the CEO type, the Politician, the Thrill Seeker, the Mr. and Mrs. Look-at-Me, and Steady Mr. Goldfinger.

The *Catalyst* would not work well with a Miser, Grand Inquisitor, Micro-Manager, or the Flake. Those you would enjoy having as clients would be Nervous Ned, the CEO type, the Politician, the Thrill Seeker, Mr. and Mrs. Look-at-Me, and Steady Mr. Goldfinger.

The *Voice of Reason* can work with 6 of the 10 profiles. You would enjoy working with the Miser, Grand Inquisitor, Nervous Ned, the CEO type, the Politician, the Micro-Manager, and Steady Mr. Goldfinger. You need to avoid the Thrill Seeker, Mr. and Mrs. Look-at-Me, and the Flakes. Also, when working with the Politician, it is important for you to ramp up your emotional expression. You want to add more flair to a presentation and exude energy and passion for your product. You want to tone down the repressed, formal nature that you are most comfortable with.

As a *Contrarian,* working with a Miser, a Micro-Manager, the Grand Inquisitor, a Flake, or a Neurotic Ned would become stressful for you. They wouldn't appreciate your true brilliance and nonconformist style. In fact, they would become very high-maintenance for you to manage as clients because your style may increase their anxiety. Stick with the CEO type, Steady Mr. Goldfinger, the Politician, the Thrill Seeker, and the Mr. and Mrs. Look-at-Me profiles. They won't be put off by your brash attitude or eccentricity. They are only concerned that you help them meet their bottom line, making money, and not the work attire that you choose to wear.

Perfectionist/Facts and Details advisors enjoy working with the Miser. In fact, if you are this type of advisor, you can work with half of the investor profiles and be perfectly content. Those would include the Grand Inquisitor, Nervous Ned, the Micro-Manager, and Steady Mr. Goldfinger. Your work with the CEO type, the Politician, the Thrill Seeker, Mr. and Mrs. Look-at-Me, and the Flake will be strained if you are not prepared to change the way you come across. Your style is to be a perfectionist and focus on detail. You experience anxiety when there is uncertainty, and are basically introverted. You will have to work on your networking ability and your package to attract these types of clients. You will need to develop thicker skin to manage the emotions of these clients when portfolios are down.

The Top Do's and Don'ts of Working with Specific Investor Profiles

Here are some key points that will help you with your communication and your overall treatment and service of your clients that fit into the various 10 categories of investor types. Through the process of understanding how your behaviors come across to others, you may begin to compensate for some of your skill deficits or character flaws. This will, in turn, benefit your clients and enhance their perception of you as a client-centered advisor who cares about them and listens to their needs.

Grand Inquisitor

If you work with the Grand Inquisitor you need to present the evidence of success (as well as the reasons why it is appropriate) for the investment solutions, advice, and products that you recommend for this client. It's helpful to the Grand Inquisitor if you use visuals such as charts, graphs, and other facts to support your statements.

Be sure to ask this client whether he has questions about possible difficult-to-understand aspects of the investment solution or product. Avoid dominating the conversation, keep the client calm and relaxed, speak at a slow pace, and be sure to maintain a pleasant environment so that your office is comfortable, and you offer coffee, tea, or some other beverage.

Whatever you do, don't steamroll him with information on products, talk too fast, give off-the-cuff answers that you are unsure of, or rush him to make a quick decision. A Grand Inquisitor will not appreciate it if you are unprepared, too businesslike or cold, or leave him confused about your investment advice or products. If you are too hard to reach by phone or e-mail, you will lose this client.

Neurotic Ned

If Neurotic Ned is your client, here are a few pointers for working with him. It is important that you present yourself as experienced and polished, and immediately provide this client with evidence of your successful track record. Neurotic Ned needs encouragement, so you need to relate to his worries about investing by explaining risk in layman's terms and focusing on the upside of investing and how it will help him achieve his financial goals. Explain the various ways you will invest to manage risk so he can sleep at night. This is all part of the process of communicating with him; in turn, it will help you build trust with Ned. Be sure to give him brochures and complete information about any investment solution or product that you suggest or sell to him. Keep in mind that while you are discussing his goals and your recommendations, try to keep the conversation light, but informative, and as personal as the situation allows. Make sure your office is comfortable.

Neurotic Ned does not like to be rushed into making a decision, and it's best not to focus or dwell on the investment risk. Do not leave loopholes in your presentation, or create ambiguity about the process of investing or about a certain product. Do not be disorganized or appear to be, and don't sound like an inexperienced advisor. Giving this client inaccurate or false information can be deadly and you will lose Neurotic Ned in an instant. The same goes for not returning his phone calls, being abrupt with him, and not attending to his feelings of uncertainty.

CEO Type

Working with a CEO-type client will keep you on your toes. This client needs to be reassured of your success record and the professional advantages of working with you, but reinforce her participation in the process while assuming you will keep her participation to a minimum, if appropriate. Be specific, formal, brief, and to the point when presenting your investment recommendations. Be sure to have concise visual and written material. Focus only on the business at hand, but provide options to this client. When you begin the meeting, ask your client how much time she can spend with you, and take copious notes during the meeting. Let her feel like she's in control, but tell her whether she is ever incorrect without offending her. Emphasize that the achievement of her goals is important to you. The CEO type will most likely have portions of her assets with other advisors or wealth managers or brokers. Sit behind your desk and wear a dark suit and formal tie. Never sit down next to her or create the context of an informal meeting.

Nothing will turn off the CEO type quicker than confrontation, or telling her she is wrong, forcing your opinions on her, and believing she will allow you to help her make a decision. Just present the information and your recommendations and that's it. Don't use fluff to describe your investment products or create ambiguity in your presentations, and be articulate and smooth while you are explaining the benefits. Try not wing it or be caught stumbling while saying, "I don't know the answer to that question." Instead, refer to other specialists on your team who can answer the question and offer a follow-up call when you have the correct answer. Other big turn-offs are to try to get her emotionally involved, get too personal, show your own emotions during a sale or in a presentation, or get sidetracked by talking about irrelevant topics. You also can't coerce this type of client into investing all of her assets with you because she doesn't want to be held captive by one advisor; she prefers spreading her investments around to other brokers, bankers, and insurance professionals. Don't be sloppy in your appearance, look disorganized, lose paperwork, or forget to return phone calls. Also, if you give the CEO type of client reason to become angry or if you show that you are angry, the client is *out of there*.

The Miser

It's a good idea to ask this client where he prefers to have the initial meeting with you. During the meeting, emphasize that you understand the importance of safe investing, and discuss his long- and short-term goals, using open-ended questions like "How are you preparing for your retirement?" and "How do you feel about investing in conservative mutual funds?" Be sure to emphasize his part in the investment process, as this will build trust. Schedule a second meeting right away to help facilitate the decision-making process. Show extreme patience in making any risky investment decisions on his behalf and discuss the pros and cons at length. Not surprisingly, he will cling to his assets. Make appropriate follow-up calls and be diligent with paperwork, and be proactive in letting him know about performance slumps. Show respect for his personal boundaries.

Two things to be aware of when working with the Miser are to never pressure him to take more risk than he is comfortable taking or to encourage him to make a quick decision about investing. If you are pushy or make an emotional plea in an attempt to change his mind about something, he is out the door. Just don't miss his early buying signals, because he doesn't display emotion in the same way other clients do. Don't try to impress him with style, flashy presentations, superficial qualities, or other phony baloney. Misers don't care. When you have conversations with the Miser, be candid, but not too chummy; he doesn't need a best friend; just a good advisor. Do not, we repeat, *do not,* forget to call him soon and frequently in the process to tell him how he is doing.

The Politician

With this type of client, it's a good idea to have a good sense of humor and be very friendly, allowing her to talk about herself, her interests, and her financial goals. You might want to open your conversation with a personal comment or question, and dream with them; this is the first step to a warm and friendly interaction. It's important to focus on the general benefits of working with you, rather than become too detailed (unless she asks). Be sure to use powerful, exciting, and sophisticated materials that will impress her during your presentation. Tell her how proud you are to have such a large high net worth client base, that you would be honored to add her to your growing list of affluent accounts, and at the end of your presentation or meeting supply her with impressive references and testimonials. If you have any good PR materials or articles in which you have been quoted, be sure to hand those out as well. Think about any special incentive or benefit you might offer to close the account.

Be very careful about being too businesslike or abrupt, and never talk down to her or try to control the conversation. That is sure to leave a bad taste in her mouth. If you discover that this client is unaware or uneducated about some of the areas of investing that you are discussing, just carefully explain without preaching or making her feel ignorant. Do not dwell on facts and figures she is not interested in; give her the information you feel is appropriate and then stop. It's a death knell to talk about the negative, to be pessimistic, or to focus too much on the downside of investing. It's a good idea to discuss her risk tolerance, but take the information and apply it without getting her turned off or skeptical. Reminder: Don't forget to laugh at her jokes and stories. She likes eye contact as well as physical contact, so don't forget to extend a hearty handshake before and after the meeting.

The Micro-Manager

This type of client will scrutinize everything you do and say. Make sure you really are on top of things when dealing with a Micro-Manager. For example, prepare for your meeting in advance and have your presentation focus on evidence and facts to support your statements, your products, your experience and skill, and your investment solutions. Have a concrete discussion about risk and how you will manage it. Remain reality-focused and on task at all times. You must be extremely proactive in servicing this type of client; that is, update him about both investment progress and investment setbacks, show him how you use cost-savings strategies for his account, and continue the discussion of both risk and reward. Keep written communication with the Micro-Manager in the file—every conversation, meeting, request, orders, and so on, along with signatures on all documents. Otherwise, this client might cause trouble—or even burn you—in the case of a misunderstanding or disagreement. The Micro-Manager should be identified and flagged as a priority to your team members and support staff. It goes without saying that you keep an impeccably neat and organized office or desk, and return all phone calls and e-mails as soon as possible.

If you plan on keeping the Micro-Manager as a client for the long term, there are a few things you should never do, including dominating the conversations or appearing too arrogant or immature. As your relationship grows, be careful not to slip into the habit of being too informal or casual with this individual; he doesn't like getting personal or delving into areas outside of business or finance. You will discredit yourself with him if you try to use humor or small talk, too. Since they are very organized people by nature, you don't want to appear disorganized, unable to find paperwork, or have a messy desk; this will drive a Micro-Manager up a wall. Don't make promises you can't keep, and if you don't have an answer to one of his questions, don't hesitate to say, "I'll get back to you with an answer when I consult a member of my team who is a specialist in that area." Since this type of client is very on top of where every dollar goes and will balance his checkbook down to the penny, don't get frustrated when he tries to account for every penny spent on your services.

The Thrill Seeker

Before taking on this type of client, it may be smart to conduct a thorough due diligence review of her finances to determine whether she has had legal or financial struggles in the past. This will help you determine where her trouble spots are, and perhaps protect you from any potential problems you may encounter. The main thing to remember about the Thrill Seeker—whether the client is a man, woman, or couple—is to focus on their dreams, aspirations, and goals, and keep the interaction light and personal. This type of individual may gravitate toward the more risky investments that have the potential to make big profits, so be particularly careful to explain all of the risks and compare them to the rewards. At the same time, demonstrate your ability to manage risk effectively. The best time to take this individual (or couple) on as a client is after the first meeting, when the Thrill Seeker is in the buying mode after understanding and appreciating the value you will provide. The Thrill Seeker enjoys outdoor meetings and other fun venues, so be sure to invite her when it's appropriate. Also, make sure that she legitimately has the capital to be making risky investments. This client will be very involved in the investment process when she is succeeding and will get hungrier and hungrier during these times. She will show you her true colors when she has noticed she is losing money. Send her quarterly progress reports and leave her proactive voicemails or letters when the portfolio is struggling. Let these communications serve as written solutions to the downturn in performance that point out your future strategies and predictions.

The Thrill Seeker will seek her thrills elsewhere if you come across as boring, too conservative in your own dress, behavior, or philosophy. No boring meetings, no boring visuals, and no dwelling on details, too many facts, or charts and graphs. It's a big mistake to leave any problems unresolved or cloudy issues not discussed, because that will encroach upon her trust in you. Don't forget to follow up with her when you say you are going to, but don't expect her to call you or return documents in a timely fashion.

Mr. and Mrs. Look-at-Me

This couple enjoys interacting with an advisor who shares their enthusiasm for art, antiques, museums, country clubs, expensive automobiles, yachts, travel, and all things cultural. Even if this isn't your thing, it's important to sound elitist and have an appreciation for these things, and share your knowledge of culture. Focus on your high net worth client success stories and discuss impressive testimonials from them. You need to make them feel like they are top priority; do this by being proactive with the servicing of their account and maintaining a high-touch aspect so they understand they are one of your top clients. Mr. and Mrs. Look-at-Me will have multiple accounts at various banks and brokerage firms, so expect that. Be sure to discuss your strategies about their long-term growth goals and how you will manage their assets to achieve these goals, leaving them to have more time to travel and so forth. It will speak volumes to them. And, perhaps, give them an opportunity to transfer new assets to you.

During the first meeting, it's critical that you don't appear sloppy, disorganized, or to have no interest in culture. Also, don't show any distaste for their lifestyle. Whatever you do, never talk down or condescend to this type of client. Don't make them feel uninformed, or like they will have to be too involved in the management of their assets. That's why they hired you. Be sure not to recommend a product or an investment solution that does not match their long-term goals exactly, or a product that is unattractive to them, even if you have explained the advantages. Don't force them, or they will take their money to your competitor.

The Flake

This client could be your worst nightmare unless you know how to manage him correctly. The first thing you should do is a proper due diligence of his background to confirm he has accurately described his assets and financial picture to you. Here is something that is imperative to understand about the Flake: Expect him to cancel appointments at the last minute. This being the case, you should pre-condition him to your schedule requirements and the type of communication (consistent) you need so you can service the account properly. Assert your control over the account in the first meeting and discuss the importance of follow-up; that is, documents, phone calls, the next meeting, and so forth. After you have him focus on the investment goals, be sure to obtain a committed time frame for his investment process. Finalize the opening of the account during that initial meeting.

A big disadvantage of working with the Flake is that you can't expect him to remember anything you told him, complete the paperwork, or even return for a second meeting. If he does manage to make it to the second meeting, he will probably not be on time, and will rarely call you back if you leave a phone message. Even so, just because *he* is unreliable, you don't want to show unreliability on your part or minimize the significance of his account. He won't be concerned about the market cycles and doesn't really want to be involved in the process of even understanding them. So try not to feel too frustrated. Also, don't forget to check on his income from time to time, because he tends to have problems on the job.

Steady Mr. Goldfinger

This individual is very hard to read because he hides his emotions, especially when he is angry. You should look for nonverbal behaviors that would indicate frustration or anger. Try initiating conversations with a polite, but personal, comment to make him feel at ease. Then present yourself in a nonthreatening way, with a gentle manner. Make your office environment warm and be sure to make eye contact, and ask about his concerns and goals, listening carefully, and asking questions. The first step is to precondition this client about the risks and rewards of each investment product, and ask him to consider investing a small amount. You will build trust this way on a step-by-step basis, and Steady Mr. Goldfinger will continue investing after he experiences each success. Then, according to his risk tolerance, suggest he take a little more risk to capture more reward, and explain your reasoning carefully. Talk about your process of managing risk. Last, but not least, a key point in dealing with this individual is to remember to ask for feedback about your work. If he is not happy for any reason (justified or not), he may just decide to surprise you with the termination of his account.

Steady Mr. Goldfinger does not like you to control the conversation, be unprepared for a meeting, be demanding, be forgetful, or under-deliver on your promises. He is not impressed with superficiality, glitter, hype, or exaggerations. You need to expect that he will take his time in making a commitment, so don't rush him into making a business or investment decision in the initial meeting. Remember, he may not even tell you he is upset or disappointed in your work, so be acutely aware of this trait if you want to keep the account.

Summary

As you can see, each client needs to be serviced differently. If you want to be able to service more diverse styles of clients, you must be aware of how you present yourself and your products to them. Once you take inventory of yourself, you can make your clients feel more comfortable with you. It is always helpful to go through all of your accounts, A book and B book, and put each client into one of these categories. Then use Act-As-If tips to prepare for meetings with them. Take a look at how you've been treating them and managing their accounts. Use these tips as a guide to noticing what things you are doing right to cater to their specialized needs and which behaviors you are not displaying. Making subtle changes in how you work with people can lead to improved satisfaction with your service, which, in turn, can lead to increased referrals. Take special note of those clients who make the hair on the back of your neck stand up when you talk to them. These are likely interactions that are more difficult for you, as detailed in the pros and cons of working with each kind of investor, as well as on the Advisor-Client Matrix (Figure 7.1).

KNOWING YOURSELF AND HOW TO COMMUNICATE WITH EACH OF THE 10 INVESTOR STYLES

	Grand Inquisitor	Neurotic Ned	CEO Type	Politician	Micro-Manager	Thrill Seeker	Mr. and Mrs. Look-at-Me	Flake	Steady Mr. Goldfinger	Miser
"THE DECISION MAKER"	−	−	+	+	−	+	+	−	+	−
"THE CATALYST"	−	+	+	+	−	+	+	−	+	−
"THE VOICE OF REASON"	+	+	+	+	+	−	−	−	+	+
"FACTS AND DETAILS"	+	+	−	−	+	−	−	−	+	+
"THE CONTRARIAN"	−	−	+	+	−	+	+	−	+	−

A plus sign (+) indicates a good working relationship.
A minus sign (−) indicates a poor working relationship.

Figure 7.1 Advisor-Client Matrix

Source: Alan Cass, Catalyst Strategies Group, New York

For these cases, it is always necessary to prepare for a communication or interaction with them by using these tips.

In the next chapter, we share a Bullish Thinking strategy with you that is so powerful you will get almost everything you need from clients, colleagues, team members, branch managers, and others by using it. It's called the H.A.R.D. – E technique—but it's easy!

CHAPTER

8

Getting What You Want and Need from Others

HOW TO USE THE H.A.R.D.–E TECHNIQUE

Now that you have reviewed the investor profiles and know your own mindset, we hope you will be able to customize your client service according to your clients' needs and personalities. By now you should understand yourself and others better, allowing you to make positive strides in dealing with stressful situations in the office, at home, and on the street.

Throughout the rat race that has always typified the financial services industry, advisors are now focusing more on maintaining a client-centric practice. They often bend over backward to address their clients' concerns, emotions, and whims. Additionally, in the office, advisors have been forced to play politician over the years to either keep their teams or their own standing in the office at status quo. Over time, those that acquiesce and give way to others' needs while walling up their own emotions may have negative outcomes for their job and physical health. Other advisors on the contrary, known playfully on Wall Street as hotheads, tend to speak up about the things they don't like, and may do it in a blunt, threatening, and off-putting way. This is why many advisors need help with asking for things they want as well as expressing in an appropriate way how they are feeling about specific job stressors. Sometimes, an advisor just needs guidance on how to

99

speak to colleagues, clients, or the manager in an assertive manner rather than in a threatening or aggressive manner. Since we understand how difficult it is for advisors to express emotions, we created the H.A.R.D. – E acronym to help you script out assertive responses on cue. We address various assertive ways in this chapter how you can obtain what you need and want—materially and emotionally—from others, specifically, colleagues, clients, and your manager. It's important to begin by considering why you may not have been successful in the past dealing with conflict. Do you have outbursts of anger and frustration at certain times that is directed at clients and colleagues? Do you have a difficult time getting your point across or having your needs met? Are you reluctant to ask for what you want out of the fear of appearing weak? Have others told you that you are too demanding and out of line when, in fact, you are simply trying to assert yourself? We get to the root of those problems by explaining the conditions and causes, and then give you the dialogue you need to assert yourself in a respectful manner and get what you want and need.

Burnout: The Beast Within

Burnout can develop, most times, as a consequence of not getting your emotional needs (achievement, recognition, support, nurturance, affiliation) met through your relationships, your career, or your community. Also, if there is an imbalance between your expectations and aspirations (particularly on the job) and your reality (actual achievement), you may go for a tailspin at work. Specifically, you are headed for trouble if there is a huge gap between what you expect and what you are actually receiving. People often experience burnout when their needs (for example, recognition, security, status, or power) have been negatively affected. Stress begins when you feel as though you have no control over outcomes and that you can't change or prevent unpleasant outcomes. You may feel powerless, you may feel helpless to ask for what you need, and that translates into personal burnout. Some equate it to spinning your wheels.

The technical definition of burnout is: A state of emotional and physical exhaustion caused by excessive and prolonged stress. It can occur when you feel overwhelmed and unable to meet constant demands. Interestingly, these demands may be from your own expectations as much as from outside sources. As the stress continues, you begin to lose the interest or motivation that led you to take on a certain role in the first place. You may experience, instead, significant anxiety and feelings of depression. Burnout reduces your productivity and saps your energy, leaving you feeling increasingly hopeless, powerless, cynical, and resentful. The paralysis burnout causes may eventually threaten your job, your relationships, and your health.

Most people do not realize that burnout has deep roots. If not dealt with early on, it can lead to anxiety, depression, and physical illnesses (headaches, ulcers, and skin conditions as well as cardiac and immune system symptoms). Because burnout doesn't happen overnight—and it's difficult to fight once you're in the middle of it—it's important to recognize its early signs and head it off. The earlier you recognize the symptoms of stress and address them, the better chance you have of avoiding burnout. There is a major difference between stress and burnout, however: While you may be well aware of being under a lot of stress, you don't always notice burnout when it happens. The symptoms of burnout—the hopelessness, the cynicism, the emotional detachment from others—can take months to surface. If your assistant, your spouse, or a team member points out changes in your attitude or behavior that are typical of burnout, listen to that person. Do not get defensive. We give the same advice to people who have a head injury; they need to listen to loved ones because they may not recognize their irritability or depression. You can't see your own golf swing—so listen. Also, what many advisors don't realize is that burnout is usually more mental than physical as far as symptoms are concerned. Here are a few symptoms and signs to be aware of:

- Frustration and powerlessness
- Uncaring (don't give a @#%%&) attitude (callous toward others and using others)
- Hopelessness
- Being drained of emotional energy—no zip, listlessness
- Detachment, withdrawal, isolation
- Feeling trapped
- Emotional exhaustion or fatigue; sleep disturbance
- Irritability
- Sadness
- Cynicism
- Increased need for mood-altering substances or activities (drugs, alcohol, shopping, gambling)

- Insomnia (trouble getting to sleep and staying asleep) or hypersomnia (excessive daytime sleepiness or prolonged nighttime sleep)

If you're burning out and the burnout expresses itself as irritability, you might find yourself snapping at clients or making snide remarks about your manager, for example. You may cry unexpectedly. If you're experiencing clinical depression, you might sleep all the time or not enough, waking early in the morning and having trouble getting back to sleep. You may be too tired to socialize. Your relationships at work and in your personal life may begin to fall apart. You may lose your normal interests, including your interest in sex. Depression also affects your self-concept (for example, "I'm useless, worthless, haven't accomplished anything"). In this scenario, you might feel incompetent or feel like a failure in general. These feelings aren't really feelings at all, but harsh, negative self-evaluations and judgments. If you reach this level of emotional distress, consult a doctor because you may require and may benefit from medication or psychotherapy.

Now take a brief inventory of your life. What are you experiencing? Are your clients disappointed or frustrated with you, raising their voices or losing their temper? Is your manager not supporting you in the way you expect her to? Are you not getting enough administrative help to deal with the increasing demands of your clients? Do you feel like you are running in slow motion, not getting anywhere? Are your team members treating you unfairly in the distribution of equity or of responsibilities? If any of these reactions are familiar to you, you may start to feel more distant from important people in your life. You may begin to treat clients less as people and more like disposable objects or become sloppy with their accounts. You may lose any real awareness of your own emotional state, and feel numb or detached. You may have trouble relating to others' worries and concerns, and don't really care to.

One of the keys that we teach in combating burnout is to challenge your sense of helplessness and to take back control of your work environment. You need not spin your wheels incessantly once you adopt our techniques for asking and getting what you want. The first step is deciding that you want to make an image change in your work setting or in the way others see you. You don't want to be considered a pushover or a hothead by those whom you might need support from later on down the road. The only way to make your mark on your office is to harness the power of using emotion sincerely and feeling to the fullest. Assertiveness is a skill for getting what you want and having your needs met and is what distinguishes top performers from banished performers.

Give yourself the power to enact change over your environment, rather than continue to be a victim of your environment. When you observe your ability to manage the outcome of an event, it can be a truly empowering feeling. When you learn a strategy to allow yourself to express your emotions and *actually be heard,* that's a powerful thing.

How to Be Heard: The H.A.R.D. - E Technique

As you know, there are four types of communication styles of asking for what you want: aggressive responses, assertive (or direct) responses, passive-aggressive responses, and passive-avoidance responses. An example of an aggressive response would be yelling at your branch manager, cursing, or making a threatening statement like, "I'm going to leave the branch if I don't get what I want." Or even if you smash your fist down on your branch manager's table to make a point, this will only create an equally aggressive response. These are ways that, obviously, are not effective in helping you get what you want. For an example of a passive-avoidance style, suppose you have a problem with your branch manager or a team member, and instead of dealing with it head on, you avoid the situation, put your head down, and continue working, never saying a word. You want to avoid conflict at all cost. The person with whom you have the problem doesn't know how you feel. Your feelings about this problem will, therefore, keep building up inside you until you can't hold them anymore. We have seen teams where people just remain aloof and nonresponsive to team members all day, leave the co-workers feeling like they are walking on eggshells around the detached person. Team members don't know they have offended you and might start finding faults with you.

An example of a passive-aggressive way of behaving would be as follows: You get an e-mail from your branch manager asking you to attend a meeting, and you either don't show up or you show up late. Or, perhaps you have a partner and in the middle of the week you say, "Look, I'm going to start a vacation tomorrow. I'll be back in a week." That's a complete slap in the face. You're trying to get a message across to that person that you're angry about something without actually saying you are angry. That offends or angers your partner and it creates tension on both sides, and no one understands why the two of you are irritated and frustrated by each other. Assertive responses are more positive.

We teach powerful Bullish Thinking strategies to help you open the lines of communication and receive positive outcomes from your conversations with others. But before we explain the various strategies, we want to clarify a few things. We have noticed that a significant number of advisors (and other people in all walks of life) believe that the only way to get someone to listen to you, or give you what you need is to be like a loud, barking bulldog. We all know people who have risen to the top through intimidation. But in the long term, you will make enemies of your friends and colleagues and fall short of having allies help guide you to success. The Bullish Thinking techniques, such as the H.A.R.D. – E, are strategic in nature. When we illustrate the *respect* portion of our technique, some may think that they are just, in fact, buttering up the other person to get what they want, and their actions will be transparent. We understand that it can appear to be that way, unless you are sincere in your actions. It's not difficult to be sincere, so take a deep breath, relax, and open your mind to the Bullish Thinking process we call the H.A.R.D. – E technique.

The term is an acronym, which, at its core, means "hard-to-use emotion." The H stands for Honest, A for Appropriate, R for Respect, D for Direct, and, of course, the E stands for Emotion: H.A.R.D. – E (see Figure 8.1). The basic premise of the technique teaches you that when you react to something or somebody, you instinctively do so on the basis of emotion and past learning, without forethought, like a football player in the heat of a game. If you use the H.A.R.D. – E technique, you will begin with identifying the appropriate time and place to have an assertive discussion about a topic that has been on your mind. You then begin the process as follows: Each letter of this acronym represents a specific element or ingredient of this strategy. Once you make sure you have all of the letters scripted out, you will learn which order to put them in when making your assertive statement.

The letter *H* means be *honest* about your feelings with the other person, and honest with how you are being made to feel by them. Think about how that person's behaviors are contributing to your feelings. "When you do *this*, I feel *that*." You must be brutally honest

ASSERTIVENESS TRAINING *RELATING ASSERTIVELY TO OTHERS*

H Be HONEST about how you feel and what you want.

A APPROPRIATE time and place. Speak in an even and modulated tone of voice.

R Show RESPECT for the other individuals' feelings and your relationship to them.

D Talk DIRECTLY to client, co-worker, manager, rather than in indirect, passive, or aggressive ways.

E Use EMOTION to disarm and verbally express the feeling that is caused by the other person.

© 2004 Catalyst Strategies Group, Inc.   FORECASTING HUMAN POTENTIAL™

Figure 8.1 H.A.R.D. – E

and upfront about what actions the other person took that offended or insulted you. You must be truthful and clear about what feeling you are experiencing as a result of that behavior and treatment of you. Sometimes, identifying how you're feeling is a tough chore; for example, sad, frustrated, minimized, disillusioned, overwhelmed, belittled. It is important to let someone know exactly what you are feeling and how he contributed to that feeling.

The letter *A* is for *appropriate,* meaning that whether you call this person on the phone or have a meeting face-to-face, you must choose an appropriate time and place. For example, you may have a client who is making it very difficult for you to complete the new account paperwork, or is not returning your calls. If this client is a doctor, for example, the most appropriate time to call her would be after hours, of course, but you can also leave a message with her assistant that shows you are being sensitive to her time: "This is Doctor Payne's financial advisor and I really need some time to talk to the doctor about a few financial matters. I'd appreciate your help in setting up a few minutes at her convenience. When you see that she has a moment, please tell her that we need to talk about something that is very important about her account." You need to modulate the tone of your voice so that it is even and calm. Loud voices can come across as being demanding or threatening and may lead to someone screaming back at you.

The letter, *R* is your assertive statement lead-in—*Respect.* Respect for the feelings of the person you are going to talk to and for your relationship with him. This is the most important element in the H.A.R.D. – E (in close second to the *E* that is the emotion). When you make any statement using the H.A.R.D. – E, you always want to lead off with respect. This approach disarms your adversary and diffuses conflictual or aggressive styles. Try giving respect to the person you either need or want something from so he can hear you loud and clear. This approach works because you begin the conversation with something positive about the person, or about your relationship with him. It allows you to empathize how he might feel in that situation or why he behaved or reacted the way he did earlier.

People on Wall Street tend to stay away from emotions and are taken off guard when someone else can empathize with how they are feeling even more than they themselves can. For example, in the case of Doctor Payne, when you have the opportunity to speak with her, you could say something like, "Well, I can imagine some of the challenges of your practice. You have patients in the office, others are calling you along with other doctors and insurance companies, it must be overwhelming at times." It is also useful to say that you have enjoyed working together over the years and how you have appreciated her insights. People are not used to having others recognize how they are feeling. That's what makes this approach disarming. Use respect and use it with sincerity and you will find it is easier to understand and appreciate where the other person is coming from. This approach is infrequently used in business transactions because of the perceived uncomfortable emotional component. But it gives you the advantage in the communication process. It will make the other person sit back and listen rather than react angrily or aggressively. If you lead with respect, there is *no* way an individual will act or counter with anger or aggression. But if you speak or act aggressively, there's a big chance you will get the same in return.

The *D* in H.A.R.D. – E stands for *Direct*. Talk directly with a firm conviction to the person you are speaking to, and if you are meeting face to face, make eye contact. Explain exactly what behavior is contributing to the way you feel and react, and what behaviors you would like to see changed in the future to improve the situation and the relationship. State clearly what steps need to be taken by the other individual to help alleviate your concerns or make you feel like you have received what you wanted or deserved. Describe what behavior change you need by being specific and direct.

The *E* remains an element of the acronym just to serve as a reminder that the core of this intervention revolves around *Emotion*. It is too often easy to forget what your goal is during this type of interaction, which is to display empathy for the other's emotions and for her to get a real sense of how you are feeling.

Then, tie a ribbon around the box. What we mean by that is that you must summarize your statement by articulating how you can work collaboratively on the current situation. For example, you might say to your client, "By working together, we can streamline the time you need to spend with me this year, and I'll have more time to concentrate on making your portfolio a success, and I'll be better able to give you excellent service." If you are talking to your branch manager, your summary statement could be something like, "If we work together on this problem and you can give me more support, my team will be more productive and that will help us meet the branch goals." Every statement is summarized with a bowtie of collaboration.

So How Do You Begin?

To implement the H.A.R.D. – E technique, you start with a plan. Be honest with your feeling and message and consider the most appropriate time to deliver the information. Respect is vital. For example, in our hypothetical scenario with Doctor Payne described earlier, the respect is in the tone of the conversation: "Dr. Payne, we've been working together for more than a year and a half, and I've been carefully managing your money. It's been a privilege to have your account. I'm trying very hard to increase your net worth. I understand and can appreciate how busy you are with your practice—you must be overwhelmed with all the calls you get on a daily basis from people who need things from you. I don't want be an additional burden on you, *but* I do want to give you excellent service."

You don't have to use every line in this statement. You can pick and choose, once you are good at streamlining this message. That conversation (beginning with the *R*) is always followed with a *but,* because this is where you're segueing in to the letter *H* for honesty and the letter *D* for direct in the H.A.R.D. – E technique. You are being honest about your feelings and what you are contributing. So, in that same dialogue with Dr. Payne, you continue with the letter *D* by being direct, "*But,* I feel anxious and frustrated when I can't discuss your account and get your directions because you are not returning my calls (or getting the paperwork in on time)." These are terms we often advise our angry advisors to use: "It makes my job much harder when you don't return my calls" *and* "I want to collaborate with you on the direction of your account" and so on.

At this point, you simply say with the *D* (be Direct) what it is you need or want: "I want you to get back to me in a more timely fashion so that I can best manage your money and put you in appropriate positions (or funds or products) so your assets will grow. We can work together to build your assets and meet your needs" (the bowtie). Or, if you are having a conversation with your branch manager, you could say something like "I'm feeling frustrated right now. I really enjoy working for you; you've been great at this branch. I know you must be dealing with other teams and their concerns. I have learned a lot working for you over the last year in this branch, *but* I feel ignored right now and a little frustrated by the fact that I can't get the administrative support that I need. I want you to find prospective assistants for me to interview for this needed position." Or, you may be discussing the needs of your team and its members. "John, I need you to put extra emphasis on my team right now because I have to fill in some gaps to increase my business. We set a goal of bringing my business from point A to point B *and* I need your help right now." This strategy makes it virtually impossible for him to react negatively. You are saying what needs to be said, using the H.A.R.D. – E technique.

It's good to remember when approaching your branch manager that the timing of the meeting or conversation that you want to have is critical (remember the *A* for Appropriate). You obviously don't want to approach your manager after a long phone conversation with a compliance officer, after someone just quit, or if he is in the middle of doing monthly reports. Simply speak with his assistant and ask for the best time to be put into his calendar. Your manager may actually be surprised that you took the time and the consideration of scheduling an appointment, and you will have piqued his interest. The smart thing about doing it that way is that you won't have the temptation to burst into his office red-hot and ready to blow up. You will have an interested and captive audience willing to hear what you have to say.

Working Together over the Long Haul

A good example of the H.A.R.D. – E technique at work was demonstrated in a group counseling session with three team members who had worked together for about 10 years, but who were having a difficult time getting along. They were all good friends, and didn't understand why they were constantly bickering and picking on one another. They knew they needed help and were eager to learn new ways of communicating with one another, but were hesitant and unsure of where to begin. To start, an individual coaching session was scheduled with each member of the team. It was then followed by a power-packed two-hour group session. We were able to discuss the various mindsets. For example, if you have a perfectionistic advisor who obsesses over fine details of business (Perfectionist/Facts and Details) paired up with an advisor who has a lax, carefree, and expansive personality like a Catalyst, sparks can fly if they can't appreciate their differences. They must learn how to manage around their strengths and weaknesses based on their divergent skill sets and how each mindset related to the others, what were the hot spots, the negative and positive points of each, and strategies of communicating.

The team, in a comfortable, nonthreatening situation, was able to communicate on an adult level and talk about issues without anyone losing his temper. After a while, each advisor was able to be honest about his feelings and say things like, "Yeah, I never really knew how you felt about that; I just assumed you were angry at the world and you didn't want to hear what I had to say, but I guess you really do." He continued his dialogue with a team member and said, "From now on, I want you to tell me when I'm acting a certain way that is unpleasant, and we should talk, because I know that I don't always say what I'm feeling when I'm angry, and I need you to pry it out of me." This type of dialogue gives permission to the teammates to actually call them on their behaviors and attitudes without going on the attack. The H.A.R.D. – E technique worked because they were in the appropriate setting, they were honest and respectful, they communicated how they felt, and they were direct in asking for what they wanted. And that's what H.A.R.D. – E is all about.

They all receive homework after the group sessions. For example, each member is doing tally sheets for the team, which are posted in a central location between their workstations. Every time a member of the team calls someone out on the fact that they have not followed through with their stated goals, the person who brings it up gets a tally point added to her score. At the end of each month, the team rewards the advisor with the most tallies. This was put in place to create accountability and to reinforce the fact that teammates need to constantly address issues throughout the day rather than put them on hold and pretend that troubling behaviors will disappear on their own.

They will continue the tallies, and once a month at our group sessions (we sometimes refer to them as family sessions because working so closely with team members can begin to feel like family) we review the tallies and how everything worked out, what could be done better, and what challenges they faced that month.

The issue to remember is this: You can have your morning meetings with your team and talk about your numbers, your accounts, and other business issues, but that doesn't really deal with these deeper team issues about how you are feeling about each other and the behaviors of the other teammates that may irritate you or make you less happy about your job. Unless you work on the intangibles to understand what is going on underneath it all, your team may be headed for a meltdown. Emotion, you see, is one of the toughest things for men and women on Wall Street to get their arms around and to identify. Advisors are *very bad* at understanding their own emotions and, even worse, *very poor* at understanding the emotions of others. Advisors say in our sessions, "For a long time, I felt like I was walking on eggshells at the office and here are the reasons, and now I understand why."

Team members, many times, do not understand or appreciate the benefits of diversity within a team. Understanding the positive benefits of a team with different skill sets and mindsets is very powerful. It is helpful to discuss why having the opposite mindset can be complementary to another, and good for business. You can use the divide-and-conquer method of profiling. Another advisor's skill strength on your team, for example, charisma and charm, may be your skill deficit; that is, you are naturally reserved and shy. The team can select which advisor is best for servicing the client, or best at capturing the assets, or better at managing the portfolios. They can also determine which team member is best suited for a particular investor (after having studied the investor profiles). Advisors may have a particular strength in one area of investing, for example, asset management, and may be better suited for a particular type of client. Others may choose to invest their client's money differently, and are not as well suited for overall management and prefer to research stocks and trade. If two advisors go into a meeting with a Politician-style investor and one is more extraverted, emotionally expressive, and verbally gifted, then that advisor should be the lead presenter in the meeting and the less demonstrative advisor should take a back seat. This situation would be reversed if the meeting were to be held with a Miser type or a Micro-manager type.

With this particular team, three mindsets were represented: A Perfectionist/Facts and Details, a Catalyst (who are polar opposites, by the way) and the Voice of Reason. If you take another look at the explanation of advisor mindsets in Chapter 6, you'll realize the reason why there was so much bickering and resentment going on within this team. The Catalyst was taking too much time off from work, and not paying attention to what other people thought of him or were saying about him. He didn't like detail work or paperwork and left it to all the others to deal with it. The Voice of Reason was becoming overwhelmed by the bickering on the team because he hated dealing with emotional conflicts at work. He wanted his team to have a professional image and thought that business was business and that petty arguments should be left out of the office. The anxiety of the Perfectionist/Facts and Details advisor was of concern to the Voice of Reason over the past months but he didn't feel comfortable opening up a conversation with him about it. He also started to resent the Catalyst because he was becoming too careless about his appearance in the office and was becoming too distracted by outside office events.

Besides considering mindsets, it's very important to understand the role that *attitude* plays within a team. To make a team *work* requires *teamwork*. How do you set aside self-interest, including your own, to fit in with the team? The only way to do this is to understand how the various mindsets contribute to the team's bottom line. In essence, a team with different mindsets won't go home together at the end of the day, so you can leave work at work. You just have to appreciate each other for what each contributes to the team and realize that you don't *have to be* best friends while working on a team. That allows for a more diverse scope or reach of clients.

The H.A.R.D. – E technique, as we mentioned earlier, is a strategy to disarm the person who you are trying to talk to. Disarm him, not in a manipulative way, but in a way that pleasantly surprises him and allows him to open up to you. We sometimes use football as an analogy: Football players are very competitive, and their emotions and aggression are unchanneled. The adrenaline gets going, and then, before you know it, there's a fight going on . . . it's how they emote and how they release their aggression. On Wall Street, the typical expression of emotion is to be verbally aggressive. Unlike on a playing field, in business, you actually have a chance to stop and think about what strategy you want to use and how you want to handle a situation. You can be angry, but you need to know to take a step back the minute the hot button is triggered, and consider any potential repercussion by responding with active aggression, passive aggression, or avoidance. You must consider the outcomes. What can you gain and what could you lose? Take a moment to reflect. Go slowly. It gets easier and easier with practice.

The H.A.R.D. – E technique does not guarantee that you will make a million dollars, or that all of your clients will suddenly become angels or that your branch manager will suddenly change his gruff personality, but it does guarantee that you will feel good about yourself. Good for having said what you felt and having asked for what you wanted. This technique is successful the majority of time when it is used correctly.

As we move into the next chapter on family therapy for advisors, you will learn that personal matters such as marriage or relationship problems, specifically, the impact of divorce and infidelity, will have a significant influence on your job. We show you how to channel a personal crisis into better productivity.

CHAPTER 9

Family Therapy for Advisors

YOUR CHALLENGES AWAY FROM THE OFFICE

In our previous chapter on the H.A.R.D. – E technique you learned to identify how others are feeling through our step-by-step process. Even though it can be difficult at first, it is possible to understand— and win over—even the most challenging individuals. The technique is disarming and allows the person with whom you are communicating to feel comfortable in telling you how they feel.

As long as you choose the appropriate time, you are honest and respectful, and then use the most direct approach in asking your questions, or for saying what you need, you have a very good chance at successful communication and getting most, if not all, of what you want from someone else, whether it be tangible or emotion-based. Remember, the *E* in the acronym H.A.R.D. – E means *emotion* and remains an element of the acronym just to serve as a reminder that the core of this intervention (or communication) revolves around emotion and how difficult it is to express it effectively. Too often, it is easy to forget what your goal is during this process, which is to express empathy for the other person's emotions and for her to get a real sense of how you are feeling as well.

In this chapter we cover challenges that you might have *away from the office*—mostly those at home, with your spouse or children—and attempt to offer therapeutic solutions so you regain your emotional stability, peace of mind, better relationships, and increased productivity.

We have found that the younger advisors and brokers (25–35) are at a level in their careers where they are trying to increase their business, the competition is increasing, the marketing and prospecting is more difficult, and servicing clients is a full-time job. All of these responsibilities, plus having a spouse and young children to care and provide for, have all of the ingredients for high stress, anxiety, worry, anger, and frustration.

Many times, it's very hard to strike a good balance between thinking about yourself and thinking about someone else's feelings (as you discovered through H.A.R.D. – E). One of the benefits of learning how to use the H.A.R.D. – E is that it will also help you identify with how your spouse or significant other is feeling, especially if you are watching for warning signs that something is wrong. As a 30-something advisor, you also may have kids that add more responsibility to your life, which affects how you think about money. If your spouse decided to leave a career and stay at home to care for the children, she is going through a major change that usually results in a major withdrawal and adjustment to a new lifestyle.

As a result, the relationship dynamics change. Most of the attention will go to the newborn or the young children. The working spouse may arrive at home anywhere from 7 P.M. to 9 P.M. after a long commute, and may need attention and recognition that may not be available to that individual. Sometimes it takes couples therapy for two people to realize that they are still *married* and not just parents. This is what it should be all about at the end of the day, enjoying your work and the people you work with, and coming home to enjoy family life. It is easy to forget the simple things that build relationships—whether at home or at work.

Being able to recognize and understand the warning signs are crucial, especially in your personal life because breakdowns in communication will occur. Both partners working long hours, not having time for children or each other, arguments escalate, resentments begin . . . these are all precursors to the breakdown of a good marriage, which can lead to divorce as well as more stress and anxiety on the job. Many would concur with the idea that men and women have different needs. Under stress, some men would rather sit alone in their living room, watch TV, and not talk about their day, whereas, many women may enjoy discussing what happened during their day. We constantly hear men vent to us in counseling sessions about how emotionally drained they are after a day of battling the markets. Anecdotally, the men tell us that they want recognition for how hard they worked, whereas women clients have requested validation in other ways, such as recognition for the dual responsibility of managing a career and caring for the children along with the running around that needs to be done for them. Validation is also important if a woman has chosen to maintain a household, keep a beautiful home, watch the children, or just the fact that she tries hard to stay in shape and in good health.

Traditionally, men want to take on the role of family provider and work hard to ensure their kids have the best opportunities for education and good social upbringing. We also have noted this level of responsibility taken by single working mothers and those who are in same-sex relationships. But these things can carry a big price tag, which drives their intensity at work that may create the Iceman. The Iceman is the individual who cannot leave the pressures of work at work and, instead, carries the emotional strains of work home at the end of the day. This individual feels like he is in a constant battle to remain afloat in a sea of thundering waves. The pressure and the intensity of work, the market fluctuations, the client agitation, disagreements with the branch manager or a team member, and arguments at home lead this individual to become emotionless; all he wants to do is just drink alcohol or smoke a joint. This is the beginning of self-medication or burnout. The Iceman tends to self-medicate with alcohol at the end of the day, which is his desired choice over communication at home, which, in turn, creates even more strife with the spouse. This action creates a rift in the marriage, and that trickles down into work activities.

Remember, all relationships are two-way streets, and we rarely assume that one partner contributes more than 50 percent to their communication problems. Always remember that it takes two to tango in any relationship, and when there is a conflict, at least one party in the dyad has to recognize it and decide to change the pace of the dance. What is notable is that open and honest communication is fundamental to a healthy relationship.

We observed eight different categories of communication difficulties in the homes of advisors:

1. *Family and friends:* conflicts about time, money, lifestyle, self-comparisons to others who are better off than you are.
2. *Child-raising:* conflicts about time, discipline, activities, perceived lack of support, lack of recognition for work, and the stress of the job.

3. *Work:* conflicts about time, preoccupation with job, bringing work home, addiction to wireless communication devices such as Blackberries, time to decompress and relax after work, remaining emotionally available.
4. *Where to live:* conflicts about location, type and cost of home, commute time to work, arguments about private schools, and quality of school districts.
5. *Sex and intimacy:* conflicts about frequency, preferences, performance, and communication. Feeling appreciated and having the energy to be present both physically and emotionally, mental preoccupation, and work anxiety contribution to sexual dysfunction, side effects of medication used to treat depression or mood disorders leading to lack of interest.
6. *Money:* conflicts about spending, saving, luxuries, investing, priorities and bank and credit charges, shopping, cars, second homes, vacation locations, and private schools for children.
7. *Drug and alcohol abuse or dependence:* When things become unmanageable at work and at home, many advisors self-medicate their anxiety or worries with alcohol, marijuana, and opiates like Vicodin to relax. This leads to an emotional numbing and an indifference to their significant others.
8. *Toothpaste:* When things are really going badly, conflict over simple daily living issues, like how to squeeze the toothpaste, may become an issue.

When a rift occurs in the relationship, one or the other may turn to an easier option that involves less commitment, less strain . . . more indulgence and a feeling of being validated: the extramarital affair or an affair outside of a committed relationship. The party who is cheating rationalizes finding someone who understands him for the moment, and compares that person to the burned-out spouse or significant other who is demanding or not understanding. Instead of trying to rectify the problems in the relationship or marriage, the individual doing the cheating makes an impulsive decision, which ends up hurting the relationship and damaging it irreparably.

Much of what takes up an advisor's week is research and face time at work, networking events, taking clients out to dinner, attending conferences, seminars, all the things necessary to build a business. The problems set in if you have a spouse who doesn't understand your work or what you do, if this person is emotionally needy, becomes demanding . . . leading one to become caught between work responsibilities and home responsibilities. He may feel as though he can't win and is being pulled in several different directions at once. That takes us back to the importance of communicating your job description early in a relationship, so the groundwork is established before you get married, have children, or make other serious commitments in a relationship.

Remember, burnout doesn't occur only on the job; it occurs in relationships, too. Burnout is simply a large *gap between your expectations and your current reality*. So, the clearer you give someone those expectations of how life with you is going and how the job may affect it, the more your spouse or significant other will be able to handle the reality later. Your marriage or relationship will be less negatively affected by the challenges of your job. It makes good sense to be very blunt and honest up front and give the other person the opportunity to accept it or not, and if she does, to also accept the ups and downs of the job as well. You might consider creating various scenarios where you can pick an appropriate time to discuss the issue of your job and how it might affect the relationship you have with that person. For example, you might have a dialogue that sounds like, "These are the things we are going to encounter in our life together. This is a job that will afford us a great deal of luxury and security if I do it right. However, this is such a difficult job, that I can't possibly be successful at it without your support and encouragement. We are a team and I will always view it that way. When I close a new account, you are a contributor to that success, because you were supportive enough to let me go after it without feeling guilty or remorseful for coming home late on certain evenings. Let's go out to dinner and celebrate together! The harder I work now, the less I will have to work and be away from home later. The more clients I can reach out to early on in my career, the more stable and secure our finances will be for the rest of our lives."

That is the beauty of the H.A.R.D. – E technique. It allows you to open the communication with another person, do it with respect and be direct, all the while remembering that emotion is at the core of the strategy. You might want to review Chapter 8 and the H.A.R.D. – E technique before you begin your discussions with your spouse or significant other.

What Is Anger, and What Provokes You?

So, what is anger? Anger is a completely normal, usually healthy emotion that, if kept in check, can lead to productive competitive behaviors at work and a great deal of motivation to succeed and will persist during stressful times. If it is not managed properly, however, it can be destructive and lead to problems at work and in your personal relationships. The intensity of anger can be measured along a continuum ranging from competitive to mild irritation to frustration to fury and rage (see Figure 9.1). These states of emotion are accompanied by both physiological and biological changes. It can also be caused by both external and internal events; for example, a client taking his money elsewhere (which is external) or if you are ruminating about your personal problems with a co-worker or significant other (which is an internal event).

Anger also can be displayed outwardly; for example, screaming, cursing, slamming down your phone, or it can be directed inwardly against oneself, usually leading to symptoms of behavioral paralysis or depression. Often, those who turn their anger inward, display it to others using passive-aggressive tactics such as being unnecessarily critical, cynical, or hostile to co-workers, clients, or significant others. All too often we hear that advisors in the workplace rock the boat rather than plan a reasonable and tactful strategy to get what they want from others. Rocking the boat may have been of use to get noticed and selected to be part of an elite firm or get a high net worth client initially, but this type of behavior can really get you into trouble at your office with your colleagues, administrative assistants, branch manager, or clients. Those who rock the boat tend to follow the contention that they are entitled to follow a completely different set of rules from everyone else. The corporate consensus reflects a belief that paying attention to feelings interferes with getting the job done. Consequently, individuals who often follow this way of existing become oblivious to the effect they are having on others. They can be judgmental of colleagues or clients who can't control their emotions, yet they themselves often fail to notice how ineffectively they vent their own anger and frustration.

We would like to show you how to enrich your life with skills on how to reduce both the painful emotions and physiological arousal that anger causes while keeping you competitive at work. You can't get rid of, or sidestep, the events or people that enrage you, nor can

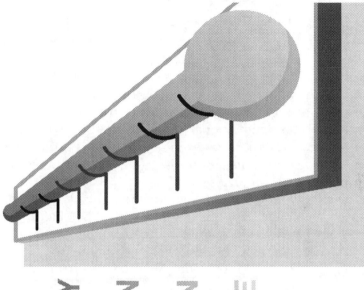

RAGE & FURY

FRUSTRATION

MILD IRRITATION

COMPETITIVE

Figure 9.1   Continuum of Anger

you change them, but you can learn to manage your perceptions and, consequently, your reactions to them.

Channeling the Anger and Rage

Much like the intervention known as Bullish Thinking, Channeled Rage was born out of the depths of Cognitive-Behavioral Therapy. We initially incorporated it into anger management seminars and workshops with corporate attorneys and eventually decided to use it uniformly for anyone experiencing intense anger. Channeled Rage monitoring logs were created to force an angry individual into thinking more about the rational facts that contributed to the emotion of anger and to think through the consequences of proactively acting out aggressively. This monitoring log allows the advisor or attorney to rate the percentage of truth (0 to 100 percent) he believes his initial angry thought to be and how realistic his new thought is after having explored evidence to the contrary. See Figure 9.2 for examples of Channeled Rage logs.

Consequently, these rational individuals will learn to adopt thoughts that are more evidence-based and truthful to guide their lives and emotions by. The goal is to defuse intense feelings of rage before it destroys a court case, a client relationship, or personal relationship that has value to you. Much like Bullish Thinking, an individual drills down on the irrational and catastrophic thoughts that created the rage in the first place. The individual then focuses on finding more rational and logical ways of perceiving a person's insult or wrongdoing so she can create a positive resolution to the conflict. The goal is to be aware of how your thoughts can determine positive or negative outcomes. Again, you are in control of how you feel!

Having to deal with the personal problems at home, and also deal with productivity demands at work is difficult at best, impossible at worst. If you get to the point where problems at home are not reconcilable, you will be on the path to increased anger and anxiety about what to do next. Once you begin thinking about subjects like divorce and the hefty price tag and sense of loss and failure that is usually associated with it, more anger and worry is layered on top of the other issues on your job. Understanding how to channel the anger and frustration will help you.

Compartmentalizing is the act of splitting an idea or concept into parts and trying to enforce thought processes that inhibit your attempt to allow these parts to mix together again in an attempt to

ANDREW the financial advisor

CHANNELED RAGE → MONITORING LOG

CATALYST STRATEGIES GROUP, INC.

	Frustrating Event	Type of Rage/Anger	Enraging Thoughts	Behavioral Outcome	Channeled Thought	Outcome
	Actual event leading to feeling of rage or anger.	**Inward:** toward self. **Outward:** toward other. Enter emotion and rate degree of rage (1–100%)	Write down reactionary thoughts that preceded the identified sensation of rage or anger. Rate belief in the reality-based nature of this thought. (1–100%)	Write down the behavioral consequence of thinking and feeling this way. Was it positive or negative?	Write a more rational way of thinking of or perceiving this situation by exploring alternative solutions. Rate belief in this channeled thought or perception of the situation. (1–100%)	**Emotional:** positive or negative **Behavioral:** positive or negative
Date	Frustrating Event	Type of Rage/Anger	Enraging Thoughts	Behavioral Outcome	Channeled Thought	Outcome
	"It's 9:30am on monday morning and my client left me a long voice mail at 8:00am that morning. He's a long-time client who has a history of micromanaging his account's performance. He stated that he's tired of doing my job for me and that he's unsatisfied and wants to take his money elsewhere."	anger – 98% frustration – 95% worry – 95% ○ Inward ☑ Outward	*"This guy is unbeatable. It's becoming too intolerable to service this guy. To call and leave a (VM). at 8:00am on a Monday morning. and threaten to take his money elsewhere. Is such a _____ move! I'm going to tell this guy off. He doesn't respect me or my assistant."* 90% Rating (1–100%)	*1. avoided return call for the day* *2. Blowing off colleagues* *3. short tempered w/ other clients* *4. anxious at home with wife* *5. argument with wife* ○ Positive ● Negative	*"I must not take this voicemail personally because he has a lot of anxiety about having so much money tied up with me. I can help him understand the ups and downs of our investment strategies historically to comfort him during* (cont'd below) 95% Rating (1–100%)	anger – 35% frustration – 30% worry – 33% **Emotional** ☑ Positive ○ Negative **Behavioral** ☑ Positive ○ Negative
		___% ___% ___% ○ Inward ○ Outward	___% Rating (1–100%)	○ Positive ○ Negative	*brief market gyrations. I will tell him assertively."* ___% Rating (1–100%)	___% ___% ___% **Emotional** ○ Positive ○ Negative **Behavioral** ○ Positive ○ Negative

© 2004 Catalyst Strategies Group, Inc.

FORECASTING HUMAN POTENTIAL™

Figure 9.2 Channeled Rage Logs

CATALYST
STRATEGIES
GROUP, INC.

CHANNELED RAGE

→ MONITORING LOG

	Frustrating Event	Type of Rage/Anger	Enraging Thoughts	Behavioral Outcome	Channeled Thought	Outcome
	Actual event leading to feeling of rage or anger.	**Inward:** toward self **Outward:** toward other. Enter emotion and rate degree of rage (1–100%)	Write down reactionary thoughts that preceded the identified sensation of rage or anger. Rate belief in the reality-based nature of this thought. (1–100%)	Write down the behavioral consequence of thinking and feeling this way. Was it positive or negative?	Write a more rational way of thinking of or perceiving this situation by exploring alternative solutions. Rate belief in this channeled thought or perception of the situation. (1–100%)	**Emotional:** positive or negative **Behavioral:** positive or negative
Date	Frustrating Event	Type of Rage/Anger	Enraging Thoughts	Behavioral Outcome	Channeled Thought	Outcome
	"My branch manager slighted me by not allocating to me enough administrative support to help me manage my accounts."	frustration – 95% / anger–95% / 95% — ☑ Inward ○ Outward	"My branch manager helps out the other top producers and never aids me. I used to get more respect before. I'm not valued here. Maybe I should leave." Rating (1–100%) 90%	1. Avoiding communication with branch manager. 2. social isolation from colleagues 3. missed appointments and calls because of lack of administration support 4. took apathy/laziness 5. yelled at administrative assistant ○ Positive ☑ Negative	"My manager has been spread very thin lately and is not getting help either from his boss. I can talk to him about my frustration and open up a dialogue with him, so that I can resolve this problem. I'm not being singled out." Rating (1–100%) 95%	frustration – 35% / anger–30% / –35% **Emotional** ☑ Positive ○ Negative **Behavioral** ☑ Positive ○ Negative
		% / % / % — ○ Inward ○ Outward	Rating (1–100%) %	○ Positive ○ Negative	Rating (1–100%) %	**Emotional** ○ Positive ○ Negative **Behavioral** ○ Positive ○ Negative

FORECASTING HUMAN POTENTIAL™

Figure 9.2 *(Continued)*

CHANNELED RAGE

→ MONITORING LOG

Frustrating Event	Type of Rage/Anger	Enraging Thoughts	Behavioral Outcome	Channeled Thought	Outcome
Actual event leading to feeling of rage or anger.	**Inward:** toward self **Outward:** toward other Enter emotion and rate degree of rage (1–100%)	Write down reactionary thoughts that preceded the identified sensation of rage or anger. Rate belief in the reality-based nature of this thought. (1–100%)	Write down the behavioral consequence of thinking and feeling this way. Was it positive or negative?	Write a more rational way of thinking of or perceiving this situation by exploring alternative solutions. Rate belief in this channeled thought or perception of the situation. (1–100%)	**Emotional:** positive or negative **Behavioral:** positive or negative

Date	Frustrating Event	Type of Rage/Anger	Enraging Thoughts	Behavioral Outcome	Channeled Thought	Outcome
☐		% % % ○ Inward ○ Outward	Rating (1–100%) 90%	○ Positive ○ Negative	Rating (1–100%) %	% % % **Emotional** ○ Positive ○ Negative **Behavioral** ○ Positive ○ Negative
☐		% % % ○ Inward ○ Outward	Rating (1–100%) %	○ Positive ○ Negative	Rating (1–100%) %	% % % **Emotional** ○ Positive ○ Negative **Behavioral** ○ Positive ○ Negative

© 2004 Catalyst Strategies Group, Inc.

FORECASTING HUMAN POTENTIAL™

Figure 9.2 (Continued)

125

simplify things. The reason for this attempt of thought control is often to make it easier to inhibit certain ideas. Compartmentalizing is a safe way to separate your painful feelings or memories from more benign and positive events in your current life. If you find out that your significant other is having an affair, this could be one of the most intense negative feelings imaginable. Once you get past the shock and denial of this, it may lead to sadness and finally anger. It is imperative to go through all of these stages to successfully overcome such a violation of your trust. Most advisors would have to make it to work with obsessive angry thoughts racing through their minds and try to remain positive. The only way to do this is to compartmentalize these feelings and bury their minds in work. Getting on the phone with clients and planning meetings with potential clients can be organizing activities to engage in. Other proactive steps would be to contact a divorce lawyer, if necessary, and maybe a therapist. The key is to remain focused on work while you are there and channel that anger, which is normal, into something of value to you. Taking back control through action will do that for you. Channeling your rage into something that helps you or your business is called sublimation; that is, a coping or defense mechanism.

We often tell our clients to imagine placing a painful memory or feeling into a box and imagine themselves burying it out in their backyard. If a problem exists at home, you must say to yourself, I am placing this problem on hold until the market closes and then I will begin to think of solutions before I get home. You have to say to yourself, "You know what, I am going to use this anger about the serious financial position this is going to put me in, and work harder to make more money." This means, of course, that you need to capture more assets to pay for legal fees, possible alimony, child support, and other things that follow divorce. You channel your anger into your business and use it as a positive thing. Say to yourself, "I am going to get back on track and turn this into the biggest month yet because I need to survive and attempt to start a new life."

It's important to talk to a friend or a trusted colleague at this time; it's a necessary outlet. You need to understand why this happened, overcome the denial, feel the anger, the sadness, and the violation. We suggest that you let your branch manager know what is happening in your life and not feel embarrassed about it, because it will affect your performance and you need to let it be known. If you talk about the emotions, and then channel and compartmentalize them, you will work through them to better understand your strengths and weaknesses at this trying time. You won't feel tempted to blow up at clients, your colleagues, team members, or branch manager at the slightest provocation. We've had advisors referred to us as clients because their branch managers wanted them, as a gift, to have this outlet. It is a gift that can allow an advisor to be productive even while going through this emotional time.

How to Channel a Crisis into Productivity

As psychologists, we have helped clients who have been victims of serious personal problems. Such problems include the loss of a family member, health concerns, financial challenges, adultery, and so forth. Everyone needs a chance to grieve and to take time to heal from these difficult issues.

Often, even before grieving, you may go through a stage of denial. Eventually you will progress into a stage of sadness and grief. After that, the sadness may even develop into strong anger and rage. The basis of the treatment is to allow yourself to feel safe with any emotion as you go through this difficult time. You often feel swindled and blindsided by the event, and the therapist's job is to offer quick and immediate solutions to help empower you. Seeking out the best counselors, therapists, lawyers, and mediators is an important first step.

In the case of adultery, you will want to explore whether the marriage is worth salvaging. It is always important to understand that, despite the affair, both parties contributed in some way to the broken marriage. Once again, impaired communication patterns are to blame for both parties, and usually lead to one spouse cheating on the other.

Sadly, financial losses may be incurred as you deal with these serious personal problems. As a result, you may return to work in a highly motivated state trying to channel your emotions back into productivity. You may dedicate a lot of energy to restarting your practice, for example. You may have more time on your hands and this often gets converted into extra meetings with clients, more marketing, and increased attendance at networking events. This dedication should lead to increased referrals and more assets under management, turning the negative, and personally upsetting situation into a positive business outcome for you.

How to Ask for Help

Asking for help is one of those things that many advisors don't do, but a candid, sensitive, and reasonable branch manager will notice the signs of anger, frustration, anxiety, and depression, especially if you are acting out of character, lose your temper over minor issues, or are withdrawn. Your manager may want to have a conversation with you if your behavior has changed substantially over time. Your branch manager may ask a question like, "How is everything at home?" It is akin to a college professor in a small classroom who notices one of the best student's grades are dropping and one of the questions college professors always asks is, "Is everything all right at home?" Oftentimes, there will be a family divorce, the death of a loved one, or a major upheaval at home, and that's the reason why the grades are slipping. The role of your branch manager is similar to that of a college professor: to be sensitive to the top performers and other ordinarily hard-working advisors with regard to subtle changes in performance or in their behavior, and calling them on it in a respectful way. If, or when, a branch manager notices aberrant behavior in an advisor, one of the best solutions is to invite him out for dinner or lunch—what we call *sitdowns*. The goal is to defuse a very uncomfortable conversation by taking it out into a public arena that makes the individual feel he or she is on neutral turf. Conversing in a public place often makes the manager appear more human and real as a person.

It may be wishful thinking, or even foolish, to think that you will be proactive and feel comfortable seeking out your branch managers to discuss your personal problems. Many believe it is comparable to admitting to weaknesses or shortcomings. We believe this is one of the crucial jobs the branch manager has to take upon himself, but we still maintain that advisors should be as proactive as possible.

If you've gone through a personal crisis, you owe it to yourself to get the extra help you need. If you don't trust—or feel comfortable with—your employee assistance program, you simply refuse to accept help from your branch manager, and you don't see any other options on the horizon, then you have to go for an outsourced therapist or outsourced coach so you will have anonymity and feel safe talking about personal matters. That will help you channel your productivity. Go to a support group for divorced men or divorced women. Co-Dependents Anonymous, Alcoholics Anonymous, and

Al-Anon are great groups for establishing support and trust. That's your responsibility to yourself. Not wanting to deal with life anymore is a serious warning sign, very much like the Iceman and his symptoms. It's a person who has lost the motivation to care about others, not desiring to look inside himself (or being afraid to) and that's why he self-medicates with drugs and alcohol.

Teams are Families, Too

If you are a member of a team, you already know that teams function like marriages in many ways, but at the end of the day, business is business and you can't let your emotions get in the way of doing your job. You absolutely should share what your challenges are at home and let your team members know whether you are going through a divorce, or some other painful transition. Your co-workers will oftentimes be happy to talk about it with you; perhaps they, too, have gone through similar experiences and can offer their support and informal advice. Also, by opening up to them about your feelings and frustrations, they will be less likely to be resentful of you if you require more time away from the office to tie up loose ends.

When someone decides to leave the team because of irreconcilable differences within it, the whole team reacts as if a death had occurred. Whether it was an administrative assistant, an investment associate, or one of the lead advisors, anyone leaving has an effect on the team as a whole. We've seen teams break up over disputes about the number of vacation days, sloppiness, conflicting investment strategies, different value systems and morals, and through significant differences in lifestyles away from the office.

If teammates have attempted to resolve their disputes with a mediator or a coach, and the result led to the dissolution of the team, all parties should go their separate ways and remember all the positives. Money and portfolios, however, are usually blown up during these team dissolutions, leaving a bad taste in everyone's mouth. It is important to look before you leap and think about the losses you may incur by leaving a team. Some healthier losses are when an advisor decides to retire and he passes his book down to a younger advisor. This can actually be a very emotionally charged scenario where the older advisor must deal with the inevitability of the situation. For the younger advisor, a feeling of anxiety and fear may be stirred up by having to take on a greater role as a leader.

As we move from personal issues involving family, team members, and the differences in response and reaction from male to female, we transition to our next chapter, which focuses on the female financial advisor, her survival skills, the challenges of working within a male-dominated industry, and how both male and female professionals can improve their working relationships.

CHAPTER 10

Gender Challenges on the Street

ROLE DISCREPANCIES

Most of us recognize Wall Street as being predominantly a male-dominated profession. It continues to be, although the numbers of women entering the business are inching up year by year for the betterment of the industry. This has become even more important as single female investors have long been underserved and are becoming more comfortable with making investment decisions. According to the Securities Industry & Financial Markets Association (SIFMA, formerly the Securities Industry Association [SIA]), more than 70 percent of investment bankers, traders, and brokers are white males, as are 80 percent of the industry's managers. The question is: Will women ever be made to feel truly comfortable to interact with their male colleagues in this business, and will they ever be truly respected outside the female mystique?

SIFMA, in its December 2005 report on Diversity Strategy, also found that women account for 44 percent of the workforce, as compared with 37 percent in 2003, which is an optimistic sign that the industry is moving toward parity with the general workforce. Comparatively speaking, the Bureau of Labor Statistics reported in September 2005 that women composed 46.4 percent of total U.S. employees, up from 28.5 percent at year end 2002. Women now represent 19 percent of the number of retail brokers, up from 16 percent from the previous study in 2003.

The industry is working hard to encourage diversity initiatives and all of the wirehouses and large retail brokerage firms are doing their share. Diversity training, networks for women, and coaching programs are all available across the board, even at many mid-size and regional firms.

But we can't deny the traditional culture of Wall Street as an old boys' network—a place so aggressive and competitive that only alpha males need apply. Some continue to liken it to a college fraternity. We know that it's not as stereotypically bad as it used to be, but there is still room for improvement. But despite the professional identity with men and the corporate constraints, many strong and talented women have worked their way to national success. These women include Jessica Bibliowicz, president and CEO of National Financial Partners; Mary Farrell, the recently retired managing director and senior investment strategist at UBS; Abigail Johnson, the president of Fidelity Investments; Mary Schapiro, chairman and CEO, NASD Regulation; Abby Joseph Cohen, partner/chief U.S. investment strategist, Goldman Sachs; and Sallie Krawcheck, CEO and chair for Citi Global Wealth Management, to name a few. It should go without saying that it wasn't without struggling and having to play dual roles: caretaker at home and tough-minded professional at work.

Challenges Being the Female Advisor

Many women professionals in this industry may have to work harder than men simply to prove something to others or to themselves, or because they must manage to be both a mother and an advisor. The first few years in production can be the most difficult. They have taken on more managerial positions than in the past, perhaps because of their inherent roles of caretaking and managing families, being the ones who can effectively organize and create harmony. This puts them on the firing line (being in managerial positions) and more problems can result. Whether or not it's true, the woman manager may get comments like "She's got a chip on her shoulder," or "She certainly is aggressive," or "If she would just start acting like herself and not like a man, we would respect her more," or "Her behavior is quite off-putting." The issue is that the female manager may be trying overcompensate for feeling like "No one is going to respect me, so I have to stand my ground and kick some butt."

It's not just a Wall Street phenomenon. The male-female struggles happen in various industries such as publishing, law, medicine, and any sales position.

Some women are hit with the double-whammy of raising a child (or children) and being there as a mom on top of training and learning the business, gathering and servicing clients, and dealing with some real or perceived gender discrimination. This can be quite a game of tug-of-war. The stress a brokerage industry job places on a family-oriented woman can be brutal. The first five years can be grueling, and some women rarely see their children. Plus, historically, the retail brokerage industry isn't well-known for its reputation of being family-friendly, as reported in a three-year study commissioned by Smith Barney and conducted by the New York–based research firm Catalyst.* The study found that "among men and women at seven leading securities firms, with comparable average ages (forty-one) and years in the industry (fourteen), sixty-nine percent of women said 'commitment to personal and family responsibilities' was a barrier to advancement at their current firm. Only fifty-three percent of men felt this way. Additionally, only fifty percent of women had children as opposed to seventy-four percent of the men, and only sixty-seven percent of the women were married as opposed to eighty-six percent of the men."

The statistics here play out our clinical experience that many of the successful women in production are either single or divorced, many with children. It's easy to see why the numbers are lower for women than for men. At some point in every woman's career, she makes a decision about her future, whether it be about having kids or the age at which she would like to be married, if at all. All of these questions must be answered at the beginning of a career, because the job description entails so much networking, traveling, and intensity that it can sometimes be difficult to manage at the same time. Many women in the industry, after a few years, begin to accept men for who they are and may become immune to their style of behaving. In a way, it can be very liberating for a woman when she can learn to sidestep verbal prods or statements that may have at one time infuriated her.

Being a woman broker or manager has its advantages, though, if she can stick it out. Because women seem to be more adept at communicating feelings and interpreting behavior, they can also use their intuition at times when dealing with colleagues or hiring advisors

---

*catalystwomen.org.

(if she is a manager). She can also use her intuition to determine various investor profiles and how to work with them (if she is a producer). The woman team member is more willing to sit the team down if it is having challenges, and discuss feelings with each member, and even not hesitate to ask the branch manager for help. And she can do this with more comfort and ease than most men. We certainly don't want to generalize or stereotype any female or male professional, but this is what we have found to be true in our counseling and training sessions. It's just the unique differences between men and women and how they approach challenging situations—it's neither good nor bad; it's just different. Obviously, there are exceptions for these behavioral differences for each gender.

Their jobs can also affect their relationships with men outside the office. For example, let's say, if a woman is successful in the brokerage environment, and she is single and establishing a relationship with a man (perhaps not in the business), and maybe she is more successful than he is. He may begin to resent that if he is not secure with himself. He also might not appreciate the fact that she needs to be more aggressive or assertive on the job and that might spill over into the relationship, damaging it.

Women and men *must* be disciplined and in control of their emotions if they are to be respected in business. This may be even more important for women, however. So, sometimes they tend to overcompensate and will force themselves to be more aggressive at work and more emotionally controlled. In doing so, they may become sticklers or so rigid that they may make examples out of advisors who do not march to their orders. They may set up meetings and discipline others more severely for having missed a meeting, interpreting it as a slight on them. And that doesn't bode well for relationships with men who may be more self-absorbed to begin with. It can create significant problems for some men because, quite naturally, they would want a woman to be more focused on them, their own career aspirations, and may feel threatened by a woman who is more into her career than into them. We have counseled and coached female advisors on how to work with different types of clients and male colleagues and we have been told by these female advisors that, for them, working with male clients is more difficult than working with women, and a lot of them have dedicated their practices to working solely with women as a result of that belief. But it can be very limiting.

Many women develop a natural inclination to enjoy working with men better than with women for the same reasons that male advisors like working with men. It's all about perception. If a woman advisor likes to work with tough CEO types because they have the same style, they will seek out these types of clients, regardless of gender.

We counsel these women who like to work only with women to take on male clients, like the CEO type, and we teach them that it is okay to step out of that comfort zone and play into some of the needs of those male clients and make them feel like they are a part of the process, like they are participating. A woman does not have to put up that wall of terror that shouts, "I'm in control; don't doubt me," which comes across as having a chip on the shoulder. So, when working with a CEO-type client who wants some form of involvement in the investment process, and wants to feel like he is making (or helping to make) decisions, you have to say, "You know what, Mr. CEO, I value your opinion on this and so let's work together— what do you think about this XYZ idea? I totally value your input." The key is to be confident enough in yourself that you can allow a male to feel like he still has a say in it and not feel like you have to control everything. It's a hard line to walk because at some level you fear you're going to lose your credibility if you show weakness, and this is more so for a woman than for a man.

Sexual Harassment: Real or Just Hypersensitivity?

We would be remiss if we didn't at least mention the decade-old Smith Barney "Boom-Boom Room" activities and lawsuits, and others that followed at Morgan Stanley, Merrill Lynch, and other major firms. These and other cases were settled and the industry now has done much to protect itself against replays of these occurrences. Sexual harassment training, gender-equity hiring practices, and other positive educational safeguards are in place. According to SIFMA, the vast majority of large and midsize firms have instituted such initiatives, and legal experts say serious abuses have been significantly curbed.

Interestingly enough, it's not just women who have been or are being sexually harassed. The Catalyst research report on "Women in the Securities Industry,"* said that when asked about the prevalence

---

*catalystwomen.org.

of harassing behaviors in their current firms, 32 percent of women and 13 percent of *men* report that they have experienced sexual harassment or work in a sexually harassing environment. Responses to the following five components of sexual harassment include:

- I receive unwelcome sexual attention at work (13 percent women; 1 percent men)
- Sexist comments are tolerated in my firm (16 percent women; 5 percent men)
- Sexual remarks are tolerated in my firm (13 percent women; 6 percent men)
- I am treated unfairly at work because of my gender (11 percent women; 3 percent men)
- Some people I work with display sexist materials (8 percent women; 4 percent men)

Emotion at Work and Home

It's important for women to save face when playing in these competitive roles. As we mentioned, women try their best not to break down, cry, or show too much emotion out of fear of appearing weak. It takes discipline and control, plus a lot of energy to mask emotion. There are plenty of times men want to put their fist through a wall, but they don't do it. We will never be able to change the culture; just as men need to learn how to manage balancing personal life with work and leaving work behind . . . so must women. And many do, and are highly successful at it.

You need to learn how to be the firm and disciplined woman at work, and be emotionally available (yes, and vulnerable) for your partner at home. It's about understanding the needs of the other person and stepping outside of your business head and compartmentalizing—the businesswoman, the spouse, the girlfriend, the mother, the sister, the adult child. If you are on a team, you must appreciate what others are going through who might be on your team, just like in a personal relationship. You must check yourself at the door each day, and remind yourself about what makes you a great advisor. Do not let gender guide your identity; focus your talents, style, and skill sets instead on targeting the right clients for yourself, regardless of gender. Remember, gender is only what you make of it. If you are sticking to the numbers and the business basics, nobody is going to fault you, and you certainly won't call attention to yourself.

Survival Skills in the Wall Street Jungle

As we mentioned, having the chip-on-the-shoulder attitude, being tough and rigid, does not create any more respect, admiration, or sense of leadership from the males who work for the female manager or who work with a female team member. If anything, it creates resentment. Let's take, for example, a female manager and discuss the best style for that person in that position. We believe the best leadership styles for a female in management is the *Voice of Reason* style. It takes the middle of the road attitude, "I'm going to be firm. I'm going to be fair. I'm going to listen to you. I am going to support you." It's a collaborative—or participative—leadership style. As a female advisor, if you have a male assistant, you must take the time to make the male feel respected and like he has decision-making power. Take the time to see if that is what he wants in the first place so resentment doesn't build. Another consideration is to know the cultural background of your teammates or advisor, because this could impact on how they view women in leadership roles. The key is to be available for all those employees around you and treat everyone the same—with respect and dignity. The branch manager or management team must be mature enough to not become emotionally reactive to an advisor who acts out in an inappropriate way. Situations must be addressed quickly, unemotionally, and fairly for every advisor regardless of gender.

Survival Skills Outside the Office

It's never been more true: there is strength in numbers. Especially for female advisors. Having other females around you to keep you grounded is healthy and important. Women friends outside of work are very important to help keep some balance between *who you once were* and *who you've become*. For example, some women who are in this business can end up forgetting who they were or what it might be like to be a woman investor because they become so closely aligned to the males, and now when they try to work and cater to women who are afraid to invest, they have forgotten how to interact with them because they are so entrenched in the male way of conducting the business.

Try to focus on each client as an individual and service her needs appropriately. You can be yourself and try to get past gender differences. Don't overthink your interactions with men because you might talk yourself out of your most successful presentation style. With other women, try to empower them, be sensitive to their needs and educate them on their options in a more understanding tone than you would for a male client. Sometimes, tone of voice and nonverbal behavior will be the subtle differences that you should look for when you work with a man as compared to a woman. You are not giving different investment advice; you are just presenting it differently to each gender.

It's important to join social, charitable, or volunteer groups with other women; to be with and have fun with other women. Have lunch with other women once or twice a week, or organize once-a-month luncheons to stay grounded. Join networking organizations and female leadership groups. Unfortunately, there are few industry groups that cater to female professionals. The Women on Wall Street Network, however, sponsored by Deutsche Bank, hosts conferences for women for leadership and business opportunities. The Financial Women's Association (FWA), founded in 1956, brings together high-achieving women from every sector of the financial world and provides a learning and networking environment. Also, the 28-year-old Wharton Women in Business offers professional development and a camaraderie for those in business, politics, and the nonprofit sector, and Wall Street women have applauded their programs.

Seeking Treatment: Don't Let Your Emotions Stop You

If you've already discussed your challenges with your branch manager (if you are an advisor) or your regional manager or OSJ (if you're a branch manager), and your attempts have not met with success, you will want to consider professional counseling or coaching. Sometimes, fear and anxiety will keep you from seeking the professional help you need, but if you are inspired enough to do so, you can begin managing your emotions and looking at counseling realistically and how it can help you move forward. Learning to use the H.A.R.D. – E skills as a woman can be one of the most powerful strategies for getting what you want the right way. Taking inventory of how you come across to others on a daily basis is very important and, most important, whether you are male or female, don't take yourself too seriously. Be brutally honest with yourself and maybe even set up a group meeting with some close colleagues to ask them how they view you. Sometimes awareness is half the battle and it's never too late to change and better yourself as a person.

Don't Mess With Me; I'm Organized, Ready, and In Control: Case Study

Miranda, a five-year female manager at a large brokerage house, comes into a counseling session and pulls out an agenda, with session goals and objectives. Very businesslike and formal. She, in essence, was completely evading showing emotion, and trying not to be vulnerable, to be emotionally safe. Of course, a therapist's office creates that feeling of vulnerability, which is not necessarily a comfortable feeling—it creates a lot of anxiety—so she compensated by trying to control the session. She took out of her briefcase two sheets of paper: one she handed to me and one copy was for her. The paper had objectives she wanted to address for the session, as well as the order in which the topics would be presented. They ranged from work issues, career goals, and conflicts with co-workers to sex life to dating and dreams. Instead of the image of being organized that she was trying to portray, it was really more indicative of how much control she needed to have over the environment, of not feeling weak and showing she was not going to be vulnerable at all; basically, not willing to give up control to allow someone else to help her.

Of course, it does show the organization that she put into it, but on a deeper level it showed she was unwilling to listen to another person's point of view and needed control over the topics being addressed. When she did that, she restricted herself from hearing other viewpoints, in a way; she was trying to assert control over the other people involved with her at the moment as well. Again, it does show she wanted to be prepared, but more than likely it was a secondary feeling to her wanting to represent herself as a star patient.

The bottom line is that she had an agenda for getting her needs met and this is encouraged in our practice. We encourage all of you to stand up for what you want from an emotional and job satisfaction standpoint. Women and men whom we see in our practices working on Wall Street are all about meeting their bottom lines and will not settle for less. That is where the genders agree.

Our last chapter wraps up the mental health illness and addiction challenges, including the hopelessness of suicide and suicidal thinking, that remain a mystery to most people. It remains a mystery, despite the fact that most everyone can admit to knowing someone who is suffering from many of the conditions we have discussed in this book. It might be yourself, or a colleague battling dark depression or addictions. We describe the suffering to you, and give you strategies to help—either yourself or someone else—before it is too late.

CHAPTER 11

You Are Not Alone

HOW TO ASK FOR THE HELP YOU NEED

You've lost some of your best clients, your spouse just asked for a divorce, and you are either too upset or too embarrassed to talk to anyone about it. So, here you sit with your head in your hands at your desk, unable to move. Or, you are in a bar, it's 10 P.M., and you've had too much to drink and dread going home. Maybe you are driving or walking around the streets in circles, having no destination in mind. You are having problems with colleagues, friends, your branch manager, your mother-in-law, everyone, in fact, everywhere you turn. You're feeling claustrophobic, as if the walls are closing in around you.

Some advisors, unfortunately, will get to this *very dark place, a depressed place,* which can happen when too many negative or stressful, overwhelming situations blanket them at once and they feel there are no choices or solutions to their problems. Disappearing from everyone and everything may go through their minds; and sometimes, thinking about taking their life as the only option. Oftentimes, this is a person's initial reaction to being flooded with stress from every different angle, but the answer is: *There is always a solution.* Never use a permanent act to solve a temporary problem. No matter what your thoughts and feelings are at the time, these stressors are only temporary. Despite your belief that they will be a permanent affliction, they are only short-lived.

Before you (or someone you know) get to this point, you must break down what seems to be a crushing rock about to fall on you by breaking it up into little pieces and analyze one problem at a time, with the knowledge and belief and certainty that such problems can always be resolved, one step at a time. Understand that there are solutions and support systems for you if you get to that very dark place. You are not alone.

So, are you thinking, "That's easy for you to say. I can't talk to my wife; I can't talk to my branch manager; I don't know where to find a counselor and I'm just going to go take the elevator to the top floor. I've had it"; or, "I'm not competent at this job. I can't handle the pressure. Nothing works out for me. I'm going to lose everything. No matter what I do, I seem to fail."? These negative self-*thoughts* can be distinguished from negative *predictions* about the environment (which may be correct) such as: "The markets are going to crash." "The bottom is going to fall out of the real estate market." "That new offering is overpriced." These judgments can be substantiated with simple questions that will serve to justify the catastrophic predictions ("The Fed is going to raise interest rates and the markets will take a hit").

The greatest risk for a troubled advisor is suicidal thinking. Advisors are expected to be upbeat, positive, and hopeful about investing and dealing with clients, and willing to manage the risks at an acceptable level. When they are depressed, anxious, or addicted, sudden changes in mood or behavior are obvious. Other signs include unexplained prolonged absences or a reduction in verbal communication. Alternatively, a troubled advisor who has been depressed for months and then dramatically improves and is cool, calm, and collected, may be at greater risk for suicidal behavior (usually because he has decided to act on his deep sense of hopelessness). He may be walking around the office wearing a mask of happiness or contentment. He must expend a tremendous amount of emotional energy to maintain this façade. Sometimes, it is this emotional drain that puts him over the edge.

These typical signs of mental illness or addiction take some careful observation. Complicating the matter is denial. Most people suffering from mental illness or addiction deny there is a problem. ("Thanks for your concern, but there is nothing to worry about; there's nothing wrong with me.") Sometimes the denial has an edge—we call it defensiveness—"You should look after your own problems before you ask me about mine." "Leave me alone, I'm fine." "Don't tell me how to live *my* life." Denial is very difficult. Blaming others (including the manager!) may also serve as a denial or distraction.

"How do you expect me to perform with these products?" "No one can hit these numbers." "I don't know what you are talking about." "If you had to work under these conditions in this market, you'd have trouble sleeping, too."

You Feelings Are Real; But Your *Thoughts* Are Deceiving You

You need to hear that when you're in that very dark place, the first thing to understand is that your thoughts are so negative or bearish that they are likely to deceive you. Your feelings are real, but your thoughts are not. You are perceiving the world as hopeless, without a possibility of ever changing the situation you are in and that there are no solutions, that you're out of options. Your mind is going to believe that type of thinking but *you have to fight against it.* You have to go against the grain to get through this period to a more realistic outlook. There are people—friends, colleagues, professionals—who actually know (or would want to know) what you are going through and can help you through this bleak time and help you sort out the agonizing feelings and the seemingly insurmountable problems. The problems can be solved. You can learn to deal with the pain, the shame, and the loss that you are feeling.

They also will help you take mental inventory of your kids and your family and how that would affect them if you actually went through with such a plan of action to hurt yourself. Think of the long-term consequences, if you can. Sometimes, writing them out will help you see and visualize the impact something like a suicide attempt will have. There are certain medications that may help give you a little boost and get you back on your game. You can try attending AA or other self-help anonymous meetings that will give you the support you need. You must give yourself enough of a fighting chance to find your options. If you get yourself in a desperate situation and absolutely cannot see your way clear to calling 911 or a counselor, or attending a group meeting, please at least reach out to your best friend, a colleague, or manager you trust.

The Darkest Place

If you are in your office now or sitting in your room reading this and you don't understand why your moods keep going up and down so quickly, and you feel like you are losing control of your mind and your emotions, you know it can be a very upsetting time. All of a sudden, the feelings of panic set in and your heart is beating out of your chest and you're sweating—that's anxiety—and you're feeling like you're losing control of your body and your mind. You may feel as though there is just too much pain, you can't go on anymore, and every day seems like a struggle. You can't continue waking up to fight this battle every day. We must tell you that there are explanations for these feelings and there are solutions.

It is possible that you may have a chemical imbalance that is perpetuated and exacerbated by real-life stress, and these stressors build up until they cripple you, leaving you feeling powerless and weak and at their mercy. So, when you have to fight a battle every day to get to work, to put on a happy face and be mainstream and pace yourself with everyone else, this can be a very overwhelming experience. You are not losing control; you are not losing your mind. You need to be very observant at this time. Think about what you are going through, and how those attempts to cope might be affecting you. You deserve help with your problems; you don't deserve to die.

When an individual gets to this stage it is very important to take inventory of who is in your life—for example, your children, parents, significant others, spouse—and visualize them. Even though you may honestly believe that others will go on with their lives after a few days if you make this impulsive decision, the truth is they will not. When you have a window of opportunity to think in a clear and logical manner, it is important to remind yourself of the pain that will be inflicted on those who love you. They will not recover as soon as you think they will. Your mind is deceiving you and your emotions and impulses will be linked to this irrational thought if you choose to believe it. We know your thinking seems so real and logical. For once in your life, doubt yourself and question the rationality of these self-destructive thoughts. Call someone and ask them for the truth before you take away your window of opportunity to get a real truthful answer. It is after all, not worth giving up and dying for a self-deception.

Mental Disorders Rear Their Head

Mental illness (particularly anxiety and depressive disorders) is on the rise in Western society. Consequently, you can be certain that at some point in your career you will meet or work with someone with a mental health problem. Addiction (drug, alcohol, and other substance abuse) is also a reality among advisors. During times of traumatic events, like catastrophe (personal and professional), war, and political unrest, substance abuse becomes a dangerous way of self-coping.* But, no one wants to be mentally ill or addicted. The culture of Wall Street appears to turn a blind eye to the abuse of alcohol and drugs. While the number of executives requiring inpatient rehabilitation seems to be on the increase, this apparent pattern *is a good thing!* It means greater recognition of the problems. These are brain diseases that often involve self-defeating powerful habits or behaviors. If change was easy, society wouldn't be faced with billions of dollars of lost productivity. These losses are the result of mental health or addiction problems that very often seem invisible in the workplace. But they are not really invisible. Astute colleagues, managers, and others pick up clues and make observations that can lead to helpful interventions (discussed later in the chapter).

Case Study: Dennis

It is safe to assume that some of our readers who may not have experienced depression themselves may have witnessed a colleague suffering from the illness, sometimes to a tragic end. Lost in grief, loneliness, broken marriages, client losses, career downturns, and addictions, some advisors try to search for meaning, but can't find it. And so it was with managed account industry pioneer, Dennis J. Bertrum, a friend and colleague to untold numbers of advisors, managers, and corporate executives.

Christopher L. Davis, president of the Money Management Institute in Washington, D.C., knew Dennis quite well and shared this story with us: "Dennis was a successful executive at a major retail brokerage firm for many years. After launching his own firm and suffering losses, he decided to go back into the retail environment that he knew so well. Unfortunately, he was turned down for a position he applied for in the private wealth management division at another well-known brokerage firm. It was a major blow and something he found difficult to accept. Things seemed to spiral out of control soon after that. Dennis took his life at age 55. His death was a

---

*See Appendix B: "Bad Medicine for Wall Street: Alcohol Use and Other Substance Abuse Trends During War and Other Catastrophic Events," by Alden Cass, John Santoro, Dave Moore, and Joseph Caverly, Catalyst Strategies Group.

major loss for our industry and for his friends, family, and colleagues. We miss him greatly and regret not being able to have helped him."

Dennis began his colorful career in the 1970s as a stock trader at the old E.F. Hutton. He was successful, and throughout his career, always had time to help a younger broker. A grand storyteller, some of his close friends say he had a long history of Jekyll and Hyde–type mood swings, and it was difficult to predict what he would sometimes say or do. Some people knew Dennis had been diagnosed with bipolar disorder, but they didn't know he had stopped taking his medication. Combine this risky factor with the job disappointment and the fact that he was twice divorced and in the process of ending a third relationship, it was easy to see (after the fact) that he was headed for disaster. It's extremely traumatic for a man in his fifties who is skilled and still has a zest for his career and for life to suddenly be like a man without a country, wandering, not knowing what to do with himself.

Is there anything or anybody that could have prevented this tragic event?

What to Do?

Sometimes, as a friend, you literally have to escort an emotionally distraught person to a psychiatrist or psychologist. Spend time with him, find out about the psychologists and psychiatrists in the area, make a list of names and say, "Let's call them right now and set up an appointment." If you are a close enough friend or colleague, you will go with him to make sure he gets there and will follow through with the appointment. Lend your support and encouragement all the way to the office waiting room.

Group or family interventions are also excellent ways to help a person in crisis. In some cases, if enough people are recognizing the warning signs (usually the family and close friends), an intervention can be scheduled in which everyone has scripted evidenced-based statements about the client's recent self-destructive behavior, saying how much that person means to each of them individually, and sharing thoughts and feelings. It can be a positive and emotionally charged environment. It doesn't end there, however. After the intervention, if the individual agrees to get help, he or she must be taken to a hospital or rehabilitation facility immediately. Just like in sales, going to treatment becomes an impulse buy on the client's part in his willingness to go along with the family's wishes. There are many residential facilities that offer comprehensive counseling and support. These facilities offer a place to decompress, and to handle problems one at a time, giving an individual appropriate space and breathing room. Remember that this type of rehabilitation is kept private and confidential and is justified for a temporary leave of absence from work. The important thing is to get help, recuperate, and come back to start anew.

When you are dealing with issues of mental health and addiction, you will no doubt enter a world of uncertainty. There are many options for treatment. The sciences of psychology and neuroscience provide continuous advances in our understanding of both mental health and addictive disorders. There are more counselors and therapists with specific experience on Wall Street and in the financial industry than ever before. Interventions by experienced staff are readily available. You should never be alone with your worries about yourself or about a colleague you are concerned about.

Case Study: Daniel

After having suffered through several years of stress, anxiety, and depression, Daniel decided to take matters into his own hands, literally, and attempted to end his life because he felt hopeless, helpless, and that his life was meaningless. He told us there was no point in living. Daniel agreed to be interviewed for this chapter because he wanted to give back to the industry by telling others who suffer from depression and suicidal ideation that there is hope. For him, it was a catharsis and confirmation that he had successfully moved on from that critical, dark phase of his life and, with professional help, is now happy and healthy. Here is Daniel's story in his own words:

> A very bad series of events occurred in my life in early 2000. The challenges began with my son, who had problems at school and difficulty in social situations. He had fits of rage, my wife and I couldn't take him anywhere in public; he had no friends. Eventually, after taking him to numerous doctors who were unable to diagnose him, a specialist gave us the news that he had Asperger's Syndrome, an illness related to autism. Even though we were relieved to finally have a diagnosis, it was extremely stressful, and it drove my wife and I apart because we couldn't agree on how to handle him. It became a very lonely existence.

Around the time of my son's diagnosis, my father, whom I was very close to and greatly admired, declined in health, suffered several heart attacks and was eventually confined to intensive care after his last major attack. His doctor told our family that he probably wouldn't survive the night and we should stay close by. When evening arrived, and I was on my way over to be with him, to my surprise, I learned that my mother had already left the hospital to go home, which left me bewildered. I was alone and holding his hand in the ICU when he died. It was more traumatic for me than I let on, given the fact that my own mother wasn't even there, and my wife was only moderately sympathetic. When I got home later that night, she didn't even hug or hold me. She was emotionally very distant (and had been for a while) that evening.

My wife (after repeated questioning by me) told me she had been having an affair with my best friend for the past two years. He also worked with me. It was more than I could bear on top of my father's death and my mother's alienation. I wound up in the hospital after a feeble attempt at trying to take my life by swallowing sleeping pills. I survived, of course, and tried to move on with my life. A little time passed, and things seemed better at home because my wife said she wanted to work on our marriage.

I was miserable, and had nowhere else to turn. I felt as though I failed as a father, failed at work, as a brother, a husband. I failed by being naïve and trusting people. Those people I trusted all betrayed me. My instincts betrayed me. I could go on living, I thought, but what's the point? Why should I continue to cause myself and others more pain? I don't want to set this kind of example for my kids. I was growing extremely depressed, although I didn't recognize it as such. I would go for long hikes and sit on a log and cry for hours. It was at that point in time that I attempted suicide again by taking an entire bottle of Ambien sleeping pills this time, and wound up in the ER again.

After my second suicide attempt, my counselors referred me to a rehab facility to get medical and psychological care. After just eight days, I tried to leave the facility and was caught. I attended group therapy and met a most unusual male patient (John) who was quite volatile and most people avoided him. During group therapy one afternoon, we were doing an exercise about putting our issues and problems in a box. When it came time for John to talk (which he rarely did), he said "I want to put my father's suicide in the box."

And then he broke down and sobbed, "Why did you do it? Why did you do this to me? Why did you put a gun to your head, pull the trigger, and never tell us why, Dad?" I immediately had a vision of my own son saying the same thing to me. The social worker said to John, "Is there anything you want to say to Daniel?" He looked me in the eye and said, "Dan, don't do it; don't do this to your son." I realized at that moment that I couldn't kill myself, that this was no longer an option because I knew that I would be doing immense harm to my child. John saved my life.

The other things that saved me were people who came forward, ones I didn't expect, who came through for me. Nice people at work, distant friends, came just to hold my hand, to visit me. This is what I carried away from that experience: if you let people, they will help you. By being there, and just by caring—it is so important.

People need to understand: If you are not suicidal yourself, but are trying to deal with someone who is, please understand that their motivation is not a selfish one, it is a feeling of helplessness and despair. You feel that your life is pointless and worthless and you are a failure and furthermore, you will *never* succeed.

It is three years later. I feel good today. I am in a wonderful relationship, and have good friends. My relationship with my kids is good. My career is back on track. But I couldn't have done it without intervention by doctors who are skilled and who are experts with issues of depression and suicide. If my story rings true for you, or someone you know, please seek help. There are other options.

The Last Word . . . The First Step

Addressing the emotional turmoil on Wall Street is not easy, and it is uncomfortable for many. But it is necessary from a mental health perspective, plus it makes good business sense. Advisors who can manage emotions, who are comfortable feeling their emotions, and who can relate to clients and their colleagues through sincere communication are more successful in the long run.

We truly believe that by sharing with the financial community positive ways of coping with the numerous challenges brokers and managers face on the job, ways that allow changes in patterns of thinking and behaving, and ways that provide relief, will result in the achievement of a healthy mindset. If the community will make these changes, advisors will be more likely to seek the counseling they need; and those who might not otherwise, will come forward to ask for help.

We trust that we were able to expose the warning signals and dangers of anxiety and depression, uncover the myths, offer practical solutions, and lead you back to a healthful (emotional and physical) state of mind. Our Bullish Thinking techniques, and the descriptive processes of learning advisor mindsets and investor profiles all work with much success in coaching sessions and in real-life situations, and we believe they will help you.

It is also our hope that the advisors needing help will find the courage to identify with others who may share the same fears, thoughts, problems, and insecurities. They will discover they may need help on a professional level and, in time, doing so will no longer be a stigma. Demystifying the taboos of mental and emotional health will help advisors get over the hurdles keeping them from achieving emotional health and peace of mind.

We want to help you find your way back to the job—and the life—you love, and to lead you there in a nonthreatening, empathic, and positive manner; to give you techniques for achieving peace of mind, more tolerance, more joy in your business, and a more balanced lifestyle. We encourage you to take the first step toward healing emotional wounds that are robbing you of a calm and joyful life and a continued successful career. Take back control of your life and enjoy even the smallest fruits of your labor. Happiness awaits if you are able to battle the Bearish Thinking. Open your mind. Open your heart. Ask for help if you need it. If you can do that, you will quiet the noise in your head so you can obtain the peace you so richly deserve.

Good luck and good health.

> The truth is that our finest moments are most likely to occur when we are feeling deeply uncomfortable, unhappy, or unfulfilled. For it is only in such moments, propelled by our discomfort, that we are likely to step out of our ruts and start searching for different ways or truer answers.
>
> — M. Scott Peck (1936–2005)
> Psychiatrist, Author, The Road Less Traveled

APPENDIX A

Dr. Alden Cass's Landmark Research Study

CASUALTIES OF WALL STREET: AN ASSESSMENT OF THE WALKING WOUNDED

Alden Cass, John Lewis, and Ed Simco

Introduction

It has long been known that Wall Street stockbrokers are exposed to highly stressful working conditions during their pursuit of affluence, which may interfere with their overall quality of life and occupational productivity. The job description for these account executives requires them to handle a great deal of personal responsibility, and because the broker is usually paid on a commission basis, he must work to make as many trades in stocks and bonds as possible to achieve success. Also, the threat of job uncertainty due to the success of online trading, the volatility of the contemporary market, the possibility of inflation or interest rate hikes, [and] international market competition . . . has further complicated the job description for the account executive working in today's market.

The ambiguity of their on-the-job decisions, coupled with the complex nature of their profession and the likelihood of experiencing failure, has facilitated a growing trend of increased personnel turnover, absenteeism, social withdrawal, and a deterioration of employees' productivity, as well as their physical and mental health (Felton and Cole, 1963; Ivancevich and Matteson, 1980; Ganster and Schaubroeck, 1991; Greenberger, Strasser, Cummings, and Dunham, 1989). These negative personal outcomes have proven to be very costly for firms over the past 20 years because of the rapid growth of psychiatric injury claims and reports of "gradual mental stress" (Lubin, 1980). Poor decision making on the buying and selling of stocks and the cost of training new employees are also speculated to be substantial costs to firms at the present time.

Ivancevich and Matteson (1980) and Cooper (2000) estimated that stress costs the U.S. economy $50–150 billion annually. A 1992 survey of 1299 full-time employees from U.S. firms pinpointed sales and service workers as being the most likely candidates of burnout (as cited in Singh, Goolsby, and Rhoads, 1994). Furthermore, the American Institute of Stress categorized the customer service worker, a position consisting of a comparable job description, as one of the 10 most stressful jobs in the United States (Miller, Annetta, Springen, Gordon, Murr, Cohen, and Drew, 1988). Consequently, a growing number of clinical psychologists have moved to organizational settings to help reduce health care costs and to facilitate interest in creating innovative stress prevention programs (Kurpius, 1985).

A paucity of research exists in the psychological and organizational literature, investigating the mental health of stockbrokers and its relationship to their success on their job, quality of life, and lifestyle habits. Speculation, as well as the findings of organizational researchers, has also intimated that stockbrokers have been overlooked as a target population for studies examining job burnout and stress tolerance (Burke, 1988), cognitive skills, job satisfaction, substance abuse, and organizational commitment. The most notable studies conducted to date in the psychological and organizational literature have investigated worker efficiency, the effects of physical and technological stressors on brokers, information processing speed, and the variables associated with increased success within the profession, respectively (Borman, Dorsey, and Ackerman, 1992; Burke, 1990; Beehr and Newman, 1978; Slovic, 1969; Ghiselli, 1969).

Because of the lack of available research conducted on the mental health, coping skills, and lifestyle habits of stockbrokers, one is left to make inferences from investigations completed on other comparable and highly stressful professions (for example, nurses, paramedics, police officers, sales representatives, lawyers, and physicians). Contemporary research on comparable professions has identified five areas of clinical concern, including high levels of job burnout, clinical and subclinical levels of depression, moderate to high levels of anxiety, stress-induced deterioration of employees' physical health, and maladaptive coping skills. Based on these aforementioned findings, it makes intuitive sense that stockbrokers may be faced with these same negative personal outcomes.

As it is well known that account executives are faced with high levels of job-related stress, the purpose of this investigation was to identify whether stress-induced clinical and subclinical levels of major depression, levels of burnout, and levels of anxiety, were present within a sample of Wall Street stockbrokers. This research sought to illuminate the extent to which Wall Street stockbrokers' job productivity (annual salary) was affected by each of the five major areas of clinical concern. We also hoped to qualitatively and quantitatively examine the coping skills and lifestyle habits that these individuals use for the purpose of alleviating job-related stress.

It was postulated that several variables, taken together, are predictive of increased job success and productivity, as defined by the participants' reported annual salary. These predictor variables are the emotional exhaustion and depersonalization components of burnout, levels of depression and anxiety, and the participants' reported number of hours of sleep per night. Furthermore, this investigation sought to differentiate which of these variables were most predictive of an increase in annual salary.

The present study used a Lifestyles Questionnaire for the purpose of identifying the various types of stress-mediating lifestyle habits and coping skills that are used by the participants. Adaptive, as opposed to maladaptive, coping skills and lifestyle habits are defined as behaviors such as exercise, proactive individual and group activities, sufficient number of hours of sleep, and less time spent engaged in work-related activities during the weekend. Maladaptive coping skills and lifestyle habits are considered to be use of cigarettes, drug use, alcohol use (more than two drinks per day), lack of exercise per week, fewer than 6 hours of sleep per night, lack of group activities during the week and weekend, and a refusal to take off work during times of illness.

Method

Participants

Participants were 26 male stockbrokers between the ages of 22 and 32 years old, with an average age of 26.27, who were identified and contacted to form a convenient sample. These individuals were obtained from seven of Wall Street's most prestigious brokerage houses. Race and ethnicity were not factors involved in selecting this particular sample of stockbrokers.

Location

All interviews were conducted after hours in public places located within the Wall Street district, where confidentiality of the participants could be strictly upheld and the work environment would not affect the participants' responses.

Instruments

The emotional exhaustion and depersonalization components of burnout were measured by the Maslach Burnout Inventory (MBI) (Maslach and Jackson, 1981, 1986). This is a 22-item self-report measure that also examines a third component of burnout, specifically personal accomplishment. The frequency that respondents experience feelings related to each subscale was assessed using a 6-point Likert scale. A high degree of emotional exhaustion and depersonalization was reflected in higher scores on each of these subscales. Levels of emotional exhaustion were categorized within ranges of 0–16 (low), 17–26 (moderate), and 27 or over (high), whereas levels of depersonalization ranged from 0–6 (low), 7–12 (moderate), and 13 or over (high). Maslach and Jackson (1986) estimated internal consistency using Cronbach's coefficient alpha and reported reliability coefficients of .90 and .79 for the emotional exhaustion and depersonalization subscales, respectively. Test-Retest reliability coefficients for the emotional exhaustion and depersonalization subscales were .82 and .60, respectively. Convergent validity was also obtained for the MBI, as presented in the manual.

Depression was measured by the Beck Depression Inventory (BDI) (Beck and Steer, 1987), which is a 21-item self-report instrument designed to assess the severity of depression in normal adults within one week of assessment. Respondents were required to select one of four statements for each item that best described the way they feel. Clinical score ranges were the following: 0–9 (normal range), 10–15 (mild depression), 16–19 (mild-moderate depression), 20–29 (moderate-severe depression), 30–63 (severe depression). Item number 8 was of particular interest to the investigators because it assessed the severity of self-critical thoughts and feelings related to making mistakes that the respondents had experienced. An alpha coefficient of .81 was found for 15 nonpsychiatric samples. This indicated that the BDI has high internal consistency in nonclinical populations. The Test-Retest reliability reported in the literature ranges from .60 to .90 for nonpsychiatric patients. Construct, concurrent, and discriminate validity are adequate and are described in the BDI manual.

Anxiety was assessed by the Trait items (21–40) of the State-Trait Anxiety Inventory (Form Y) (STAI) (Spielberger, Gorsuch, and Lushene, 1970). These 20 items were used to evaluate how respondents generally feel in a variety of hypothetical situations. The essential symptoms assessed by this instrument are feelings of apprehension, tension, nervousness, and worry. The higher the accumulated score on this inventory, the more severe was the anxiety experienced by the respondent. The cutoff score prescribed by the authors to differentiate those working adults (n = 1,387) who are highly anxious from those who experience normal levels of anxiety, was set at 44.08. More than 5,000 subjects were tested in the construction and standardization of the STAI. Alpha coefficients are reported to be .91 for working adults. Evidence for the concurrent, convergent, divergent, and construct validity of the STAI is present and displayed in the manual.

Clinical and subclinical levels of current major depression were determined through the use of the Structured Clinical Interview for DSM-IV (SCID) (First, Spitzer, Gibbon, and Williams, 1994). This instrument was used to make an accurate assessment of whether each participant met DSM-IV criteria for clinical or subclinical levels of current major depression. An individual responded to the verbally presented criteria regarding the presence of symptoms of depression, while the examiner coded each response as a 1 (absent symptom), 2 (subthreshold or subclinically present symptom), or 3 (threshold, clinically present symptom). This instrument has not been used within organizational settings to date, but was useful in making more of an accurate diagnosis at the time of each interview.

An individual must first have experienced within the past month, either two weeks of a depressed mood for most of the day or two weeks of markedly diminished interest or pleasure in almost all activities most of the day to be diagnosed with current Major Depressive Disorder using this instrument. If the examiner coded at least one of these first two symptoms as being clinically present (3), then the individual was required to report clinically present symptoms (3) for at least four more of the next seven items presented to them. (Please refer to DSM-IV criteria for Current Major Depression criteria A3–A9). Thus, at least five of the presented symptoms must be coded a (3) and at least one of these must be item 1 or 2. If this requirement was met, then the individual must be coded a (3), attesting to the fact that these symptoms caused him clinically significant distress or impairment in social, occupational, or other important areas of functioning. If this requirement was satisfied, the next step was taken toward a diagnosis if a (3) is coded for criteria ruling out depression due to the physiological effects of a substance or due to a general medical condition. Finally, the diagnosis could be made for clinical levels of current Major Depressive Disorder if the individual was coded a (3) for a response ruling out depression due to bereavement. Any individual who was coded with at least one (3) for the first two items, but did not meet criteria for clinical levels of current Major Depressive Disorder, was coded as a (2), signifying subclinical levels of depression.

Relevant qualitative information about the participants was obtained by using a tailor-made Demographics Questionnaire. This questionnaire required that the participants report information regarding their age, years at their current occupation, level of education, socioeconomic status, estimated annual salary, previous occupation, number of hours in the office per day, previous psychiatric hospitalizations, level of education, and marital status. This questionnaire was used solely for this initial investigation on stockbrokers and thus, reliability and validity statistics are not currently available.

Finally, a brief Lifestyles and Coping skills questionnaire was created to determine whether these participants were using adaptive or maladaptive coping skills as a means of relieving stress. Participants were required to fill in blanks at the end of a posed question, with personal and qualitative information regarding their lifestyle habits and coping skills. Specific areas of interest were tapped through the use of this questionnaire, such as the number of hours during the week and weekends spent in individual or group activities, the types of activities used to alleviate stress, consumption behaviors (for example, alcohol, cigarette, and drug use), sleeping habits, and physical health. No reliability or validity data can be presented for this questionnaire, as it has not been used in any previous investigations that focused on this population of professionals.

The readability and comprehension of this questionnaire was checked by administering the questionnaire to several adult males during a pilot investigation.

Procedure

Institutional Review Board (I.R.B.) approval was obtained before submitting the study. All subjects were treated according to APA guidelines for the ethical treatment of human subjects.

The examiner used standardized procedures throughout each assessment, and in all cases, the order of the instruments used was maintained (Demographics Questionnaire, Lifestyles Questionnaire, MBI, Trait items from STAI (Form Y), BDI, SCID oral interview). Each assessment packet was coded with a number that was assigned to the participant for the purpose of insuring anonymity. Participants completed the self-report questionnaires without the guidance of the examiner, and when they were completed, these questionnaires were collected. At this point, the examiner informed the participants that they would be tape-recorded and asked to respond orally to questions about their mood within the last month (SCID, 1994). Following this structured clinical interview, participants were debriefed and informed of their right to request information regarding the results of the study. Participants were thanked and asked not to discuss the experience with their co-workers. The total procedure required 30 minutes in most cases, but for those not meeting criteria for either subclinical or clinical levels of Major Depression on the SCID, the procedure took only 20 minutes.

Once the data were collected, the examiner used the SPSS 9.0 for Windows program to enter it into analyses of interest such as Multiple Regression analysis, ANOVA, and descriptive statistics.

Results

Before conducting the multiple regression analysis, regression diagnostics were performed on the data to determine the degree to which the assumptions of multiple regression were met. This analysis was also conducted to discover whether the variables, emotional exhaustion, depersonalization, depression and trait-anxiety levels, and the number of hours of sleep per night, taken together, could significantly predict how successful a stockbroker would be, as measured by his reported annual salary. This statistical analysis yielded results indicating that these aforementioned variables, as a group, were significantly predictive of the participants' reported annual salary ($R = .667$, $p < .05$). Together, these five predictor variables account for 30.6 percent of the variance in reported annual salary ($R2 = .445$, adjusted $R2 = .306$, $F(5,20) = 3.204$, $p < .05$).

Results suggested that only two of these five variables, depersonalization levels and hours of sleep, were independently and significantly related to the outcome measure under investigation. The Beta weights (standardized multiple regression coefficients) and squared semipartial regression coefficients (uniqueness index) were also reviewed to assess the relative contribution of the five variables to the prediction of job success, as measured by reported annual salary.

Specifically, the depersonalization variable displayed the largest significant standardized weight and the second largest significant squared semipartial regression coefficient, with values of $-.56$ ($p < .05$) and .1946, respectively. The Pearson correlation coefficient was found to be in the predicted direction, and supported prior findings that identified a negative relationship between job success and levels of depersonalization. Lower levels of depersonalization were thus moderately associated with an increase in job success or reported annual salary ($r = -.467$, $p < .05$). The findings regarding squared semipartial regression coefficients indicated that depersonalization accounted for approximately 19 percent of the variable in annual salary, beyond the variance accounted for by the other four predictors.

In addition to the negative relationship discovered with depersonalization, annual salary was expected to have a positive relationship with the number of hours of sleep per night. Contrary to prior research findings that pinpointed negative personal outcomes related to sleep deprivation, however, it appeared that the variable for number of hours of sleep was negatively related to the annual salary of the participants, as evidenced by a Pearson correlation coefficient of $-.453$. This variable also displayed a significant standardized weight at a value of $-.52$ ($p < .05$), indicating the strength of its relative contribution to the prediction of reported annual salary. The findings regarding uniqueness were also significant in that the number of hours of sleep variable accounted for approximately 23 percent of the variable in reported annual salary, beyond the variance accounted for by the other four predictors ($Sr2 = .2304$).

The results of this investigation also yielded descriptive data regarding the samples' scores on several mental health assessments (BDI, Trait Anxiety Inventory, MBI, SCID), as well as on their lifestyle habits and coping skills (Lifestyles Questionnaire). Means and standard deviations for both sets of data appear in Tables A.1 and A.2.

Table A.1:   Descriptive Statistics

Mental Health Indicators

	Mean	Standard Deviation
Emotional Exhaustion	24.92	9.45
Depersonalization	11.42	6.67
SCID Current Depression	1.81	.80
Trait Anxiety Raw Scores	41.31	7.58
BDI-Depression Raw Scores	9.69	6.86

Table A.2:   Descriptive Statistics

Lifestyles Habits and Coping Skills

	Mean	Standard Deviation
Years at current job	2.69	1.98
Annual salary*	$139†	$130†
Hours at work	10.27	1.22
Hours of work on weekends	2.42	2.02
Hours of individual activities (week)	8.46	6.82
Hours of group activities (week)	5.85	7.15
Hours of individual activities (weekends)	7.65	9.71
Hours of group activities (weekends)	9.19	7.90
Number of alcoholic drinks	1.50	1.63
Hours of exercise	5.15	5.18
Packs of cigarettes per day	1.54	.51
Drug use quantity per week	2.58	3.58
Hours of sleep	6.23	1.82
Time to fall asleep (minutes)	36.54	30.91
Days of illness	4.15	3.45
Sick day absenteeism	2.23	2.41
BDI-Item 8 (self-critical thoughts)	.96	.53

*The median annual salary for this sample was found to be $100,000.
†Expressed as thousands

Discussion

This preliminary investigation examined the relationship of five variables, all of which have been associated with negative emotional and physical outcomes, and their ability to predict the job success of 26 Wall Street stockbrokers. Although as a group, these five predictor variables were shown to be significantly related to the reported annual salary of the participants, it was surprising that only depersonalization levels and the number of hours of sleep variables contributed to the majority of this relationship.

Corroborating earlier research conducted by Maslach (1982), there was evidence of a significant and moderate relationship, in a predicted direction, between levels of depersonalization and the reported annual salary of the stockbrokers. It was expected that stockbrokers, who used depersonalization as an emotional buffer and to psychologically distance themselves from their clients, would report having lower annual salaries within this sales-related profession. It may be that stockbrokers, facing high levels of depersonalization, treated their clients in a predictably cold and unfriendly manner. Clients may consequently have taken their accounts elsewhere. It is therefore plausible that the stockbrokers may have greater earning potential if they learn to be more expressive and aware of their emotions, and begin to treat their clients in a more personal and concerned manner. It is also speculated that higher levels of depersonalization may decrease an individual's awareness of their own psychological and physical health. This lack of awareness may lead one to engage in poor lifestyle habits and use ineffective coping skills, both of which may affect an individual's ability to be productive at work, as well as affect their mental and physical health.

The second variable, the number of hours of sleep per night, was found to be significantly and negatively related to job success. These results suggest that those stockbrokers who spent less time sleeping each night are more likely to have a higher annual salary. This makes intuitive sense in that sleeping less would give a stockbroker more time to research new stocks and obtain new accounts while at work and home. Consequently, more time devoted to work and less to sleep would increase the likelihood of reaching a higher annual salary.

Contemporary literature, however, has shown that negative psychological and physical outcomes have been associated with a lack of sleep (Kahill, 1988). This relationship between a lack of sleep and negative personal outcomes validated our contention that these individuals may neglect their physical and mental health, possibly as a result of experiencing moderate to high levels of depersonalization, or as a means of pursuing affluence in an extremely volatile stock market.

The results of this study indicated that trait anxiety, levels of depression, and emotional exhaustion were not large contributors to the prediction of annual salary. This finding is intriguing in that prior research, as well as intuitive sense, would lead one to hypothesize a strong negative relationship between these three variables and an individual's success on the job. One reason for this may be that the brokers within our sample may have been experiencing high levels of depersonalization, and consequently, were not even aware of their symptoms of depression, anxiety, and emotional exhaustion for them to subscribe to in the self-reports. This finding may be worth exploring in future investigations.

The descriptive data obtained through the use of our assessment questionnaires contributed to the investigators' understanding of the current mental health, coping skills, and lifestyle habits of these 26 stockbrokers. The results reported in Table A.1 lend credence to our contention that the mental health and quality of life of stockbrokers is negatively affected by high levels of job-related stress. Most notably, the results indicated that the participants' obtained mean scores placed them in the moderate-to-high range for emotional exhaustion and depersonalization. Regarding the levels of trait anxiety on the STAI, the stockbrokers obtained a mean score that was higher than the mean obtained by the original norm group ($41.31 > 34.89$) that was composed of working adults (Spielberger, Gorsuch, and Lushene, 1970). The original STAI standardization sample was not composed of stockbrokers, suggesting that the present sample may be faced with qualitatively and quantitatively different types of job-related stressors. The results, however, indicated that the respondents for our investigation reported significant amounts of distress related to symptoms of anxiety. Finally, regarding the participants' acknowledgment of depressive symptoms, results obtained from the BDI and SCID instruments suggested that, on the average, they approached mild levels of depression and subclinical levels of Current Major Depression, respectively.

Means and standard deviations of items on the Lifestyles Questionnaire indicated that the stockbrokers were using some maladaptive coping skills and were engaged in some risky lifestyle habits during the workweek. Specifically, these individuals were spending between 10 to 12 hours at work, smoked on average almost two packs of cigarettes, and consumed almost two drinks each day. This sample also reported, on the average, using both alcohol and some form of illegal substance at least two times. Relating to sleep patterns, these individuals on the average took almost 37 minutes per night to fall asleep, leaving them with about six hours of sleep for the rest of the night. Regarding their awareness of their physical health, these individuals reported suffering from either the flu or a virus, on the average, four times per year, and still only called in sick for work two times, indicating either the extent of their motivation or fear of not being at work. The stockbrokers within our sample also showed evidence of negativistic thought patterns, in that approximately 96 percent of them agreed with the BDI statement "I am critical of myself for my weaknesses and mistakes." Finally, these individuals chose to engage in more pleasurable individual activities (for example, jogging, fishing, masturbation) than group activities (for example, drinks with friends, going to dinner, sex, nightclubs with friends) during the week and more pleasurable group activities than individual ones during their weekends.

It was our contention that stockbrokers were a population of professionals facing high levels of job-related stress, and that this stress, if not actively mediated, would impair their mental and physical health as well as their occupational and social functioning. The results of our investigation illuminated the fact that our participants, on average, were experiencing moderate-to-high levels of depersonalization and emotional exhaustion, both of which compose two-thirds of job burnout (Maslach, 1982). These individuals were also certainly reporting a moderate-to-high level of distress relating to manifestations of anxiety, as well as mild depressive symptoms.

Although the participants reached only mild levels of depression on the face valid BDI measure, it was fortuitous that we used a structured interview (SCID) (First et al., 1994) for the purpose of identifying clinical, as well as subclinical levels of Current Major Depression within this sample. The results indicated that 23 percent of our sample met criteria for a clinical diagnosis of Current Major Depression and 38 percent reached criteria for subclinical levels. This finding is startling because the National Institute of Mental Health (2000) has reported that 7 percent of all men are currently diagnosed with major depression, and our sample of males contains a much greater percentage of depression than that would be expected in the general population at the present time. Thus, many of these individuals may require professional help and perhaps even medication to alleviate their distress, but they are not likely to seek the help necessary to ameliorate these symptoms.

The most astounding finding of our investigation is that despite the moderate-to-high levels of emotional distress reported by the participants, these individuals were still making on average $139,346.15 for their annual income. Even more surprising was the revelation that those brokers who reported greater impairment regarding depression, anxiety, and emotional exhaustion, as well as poorer coping skills, proved to be the most successful individuals within our sample on the basis of their annual income. In essence, these rookie brokers appear to be paying for financial success with their mental health and their quality of life.

The results of this investigation have implications for the provision of services in organizational settings to the increasing number of employees who experience clinically significant work-related stress and are at risk for mental illness, physical impairment, and burnout. It appears that stockbrokers are not using effective coping skills for the purpose of alleviating their work-related stress, and consequently, are developing the debilitating symptoms of burnout, anxiety, and depression. It is our contention that negative personal outcomes will be associated with these mental health concerns, and will consequently lead to negative organizational outcomes such as absenteeism and a decreased quality of life for employees and their families. Also, if the early warning signs of burnout, depression, and anxiety continue to remain unnoticed by stockbrokers as well as their employers, their overall productivity and commitment to the organization may wane over time, leading to an increase in turnover. This may cost brokerage houses additional money for training replacement brokers who will more than likely suffer the same fate as their predecessors.

The present investigation thus sheds light on the importance of preventing mental and physical illness from infringing on the lives of stockbrokers. It behooves the larger organizations to implement some form of stress management program at a training level for the purpose of preventing these rather costly and negative personal outcomes from affecting their employees, and eventually the growth of the organization. As clinical stress researchers, we concur with the work of Lazarus and Folkman (1984), and consequently emphasize the importance of continued organizational research on individuals and how they perceive or appraise the stressors within the working environment. It appears that a great deal of energy is currently being directed toward identifying environmental triggers within organizations that elicit stress within employees. Not a lot of research is required, unfortunately, to realize that for the stockbroker, the environmental stressor that most significantly contributes to the increased levels of burnout, depression, anxiety, and poor coping skills is the ambiguous and intangible stock market. This particular stressor cannot be eliminated from their job description, which means that a more person-centered focus is required for organizational researchers who study stockbrokers. Early interventions during training will hopefully enable these individuals to identify means to turn perceived threats into perceived challenges, and improve their overall quality of life.

References

Beck, A.T., and Steer, R.A. 1987. *Beck Depression Inventory*. San Antonio, TX: Psychological Corporation/Harcourt Brace Jovanovich.

Beehr, T.A., and Newman, J.E. 1978. Job stress, employee health, and organizational effectiveness: A facet analysis, model and literature review. *Personnel Psychology*, 31:665–699.

Borman, W.C., Dorsey, D., and Ackerman, L. 1992. Time-spent responses as time allocation strategies: Relations with sales performance in a stockbroker sample. *Personnel Psychology*, 45:763–777.

Burke, R.J. "Sources of managerial and professional stress in large organizations." 1988. In *Courses, coping and consequences of stress at work*, by C.L. Cooper and R. Payne (eds.), 77–114. Hoboken, NJ: Wiley.

Burke, R.J. 1990. Effects of physical environment and technological stressors among stock brokers: A preliminary investigation. *Psychological Reports*, 66:951–959.

Cooper, C.L. 2000. Editorial: Future research in occupational stress. *Stress Medicine*, 16:63–64.

Felton, J.S., and Cole, R. 1963. The high cost of heart disease. *Circulation*, 27:957–962.

First, M., Spitzer, R.L., Gibbon, M., and Williams, J.B.W. 1994. *Structured Clinical Interview for DSM-IV*, Washington, D.C.: American Psychiatric Association.

Ganster, D.C., and Schaubroeck, J. 1991. Work stress and employee health. *Journal of Management*, 17(2):235–271.

Ghiselli, E.E. 1969. Prediction of success of stockbrokers. *Personnel Psychology*, 22:125–130.

Greenberger, D.B., Strasser, S., Cummings, L.L., and Dunham, R.B. 1989. The impact of personal control on performance and satisfaction. *Organizational Behavior and Human Decision Processes*, 43:29–51.

Ivancevich, J.M., and Matteson, M.T. 1980. *Stress and work: A managerial perspective.* Glenview, IL: Scott, Foresman.

Kahill, S. 1988. Symptoms of professional burnout: A review of the empirical evidence. *Canadian Psychology/Psychologie Canadienne,* 29(3):284–297.

Kurpius, D. 1985. Consultation interventions: Successes, failures, and proposals. *The Counseling Psychologist,* 13:368–389.

Lazarus, R.S., and Folkman, S. 1984. *Stress, appraisal, and coping.* New York: Springer.

Lubin, J. "On-the-job stress leads many workers to file—and win—compensation awards." *Wall Street Journal* (September 17, 1980), B1.

Maslach, C., and Jackson, S.E. 1981. The measurement of experienced burnout. *Journal of Occupational Behavior,* 2:99–113.

Maslach, C. 1982. *Burnout: The cost of caring.* Englewood Cliffs, NJ: Prentice-Hall.

Maslach, C., and Jackson, S.E. 1986. *The Maslach Burnout Inventory.* Palo Alto, CA: Consulting Psychologists Press.

Miller, A., Springen, K., Gordon, J., Murr, A., Cohen, B., and Drew, L. "Stress on the Job." *Newsweek* (April 25, 1988), 40–45.

National Institute of Mental Health Survey 2000, Report obtained online: nimh.nih.gov.

Singh, J., Goolsby, J.R., and Rhoads, G.K. 1994. Behavioral and psychological consequences of boundary spanning burnout for customer service representatives. *Journal of Marketing Research,* 31:558–565.

Slovic, P. 1969. Analyzing the expert judge: A descriptive study of a stockbroker's decision processes. *Journal of Applied Psychology,* 53(4):255–263.

Spielberger, C.D., Gorsuch, R.L., and Lushene, R.E. 1970. *Manual for the State-Trait Anxiety Inventory.* Palo Alto, CA: Consulting Psychologists Press.

APPENDIX B

Bad Medicine for Wall Street

ALCOHOL USE AND OTHER SUBSTANCE ABUSE TRENDS DURING WAR AND OTHER CATASTROPHIC EVENTS

Alden Cass, Joseph Santoro, Dave Moore, and Joseph Caverly

Abstract

There is a body of evidence indicating that uncontrollable traumatic events can contribute to an increased susceptibility in alcohol use (National Institute on Drug Abuse, 2002; Volpicelli et al., 1999). Research has also supported the notion that alcohol consumption and traumatic events are related, with the most pronounced increase in alcohol use following the trauma, rather than during the actual event (Volpicelli et al., 1990). As traumatic events typically elicit strong emotional reactions in humans, self-medication through alcohol use has served as a prominent coping mechanism to decrease painful affect (Epstein et al., 1998).

There is a common perception among business executives of a stigma attached to weakness or painful feelings. Business executives are consequently reticent to respond to alcohol use surveys for fear their jobs will be threatened if they are truthful in responding. A confidential alcohol use survey using the Alcohol Use Disorders Identification Test (AUDIT) and a demographics questionnaire examining participants' gender, age, income levels, marital status, company location, and type of job were conducted through the Internet to encourage truthful responding.

A total of 151 usable surveys were collected and analyzed. The majority of participants were single men under the age of 30 who do not exercise frequently and made less than $100,000 per year. To examine the findings of the current study, an analysis of variances (ANOVAs) and t-tests were performed to determine whether significant differences in problematic drinking behaviors occurred across the pre-, during, and postwar groups. Interestingly, the findings refuted the *happy hour effect* (Volpicelli et al., 1990), with significantly more problematic drinking behaviors occurring during than after the war. Also, participants from the during-war group drank more often, binge drank more, and felt more guilt and remorse after drinking.

Bad Medicine for Wall Street: Alcohol Use Trends During War

Mental health professionals universally consider alcohol and drug addictions to be severe and pervasive problems, spanning across several areas of modern society. Substance abuse affects millions of Americans each day and costs society billions of dollars per year in treatment and prevention efforts. Substance abuse has been the subject of hundreds of research studies over the years, but certain populations have been excluded from these studies. Wall Street executives have been largely underserved and ignored with respect to their mental health and substance abuse concerns. The issues of mental illness and substance abuse have also been linked to a stigma of weakness and passivity in corporate America.

The issue of substance abuse is speculated to be sidestepped or conveniently ignored by most financial services companies until an employee begins to display problems with his overall productivity, thus negatively affecting the bottom line of a company. Many employees may feel that alcohol use is part of the corporate culture for networking, making business transactions, and relaxation. Alcohol use problems are rarely talked about, and when they are, employees may feel that their jobs are in jeopardy if management were to find out. For this reason, an Internet investigation was utilized to allow these individuals to honestly and anonymously answer questions about their alcohol use in a safe and confidential manner.

The current study was developed as a result of a paucity of research available concerning mental health and substance abuse concerns facing Wall Street executives (Cass et al., 2000). The focus of this investigation is on the impact of the United States's involvement in Iraq in response to September 11th on Wall Street executives with regard to their alcohol abuse patterns and job performance. Specifically, this study examined whether the stress in anticipation of the war, during the war period, or after the declared end of the war influenced alcohol use problems among financial services executives.

Trauma and stress have been linked to the development of alcoholism and other substance abuse problems (Brady and Sonne, 1999; Crum, Muntaner, Eaton, and Anthony, 1995; Najavits, Weiss, and Shaw, 1997; Najavits, Weiss, and Shaw, 1999; Seeman and Seeman, 1992; Volpicelli, Balaraman, Hahn, Wallace, and Bux, 1999) with significant impact on multiple areas of a person's life. Alcoholism often diminishes work performance, family relationships, legal standing, and a host of other life situations that are considered to be vital to daily living. The severity of trauma and stress has been positively correlated to the likelihood of developing a substance abuse disorder (Brown and Anderson, 1991; Fullilove, Fullilove, Smith, Winkler, Micheal, Panzer, and Wallace, 1993). In general, it was found that the greater the violence experienced and the greater the number of violent experiences, the greater the likelihood of developing a substance abuse disorder. The trauma experienced both directly and vicariously by people in and around the Wall Street district on September 11, 2001, was likely a very traumatic event in their lives.

In a large survey of males, Seeman and Seeman (1992) found that drinking problems were closely related to stressful experiences. Their research indicated that such experiences did not need to be severe or chronic to produce a drinking problem. The event could be related to an occupational stressor in which the person feels powerless, and thus uses alcohol as a coping mechanism. Male participants in the Seeman study reported the most severe drinking problems developed in response to an occupational stressor of not having the freedom to choose how to fulfill their job obligations. The lack of control and freedom to choose seems to be a risk factor for the development of drinking problems in the workplace.

Crum et al. (1995) also found that the type of stress experienced has an impact on whether a person will develop a dependence on alcohol. Their study looked at men in high-strain (high demand and low control) and low-strain (low demand and high control) job situations. They found that men in high-strain jobs were more likely to develop an alcohol dependence than men in low-strain jobs. In a related study, Takeshita, Muruyama, and Morimoto (1998), found that chronic, low level, work-related stressors are associated with higher drinking levels. An example of this type of stressor would be dealing with an uncooperative co-worker or daily parking problems at the office. The employee often has limited control over the outcome of the situation and feels frustrated. This research again makes the case for control being a major risk factor in the development of alcoholism.

Volpicelli et al. (1999) have done extensive work on trauma, Post-Traumatic Stress Disorder (PTSD), and alcohol addictions. Specifically, they have investigated the role that uncontrollable trauma plays in the development of PTSD and alcohol addictions. The degree to which a person can control a traumatic event is an important factor in understanding the impact of the event (Maier and Seligmanm, 1975) and the subsequent development of PTSD or alcoholism. If a person is unable to control a traumatic event, he is more likely to act passively and fearfully in similar situations. This sets the person up for the development of PTSD-like symptoms. In response to these feelings, people often self-medicate with alcohol to avoid emotional distress related to the trauma (Volpicelli et al., 1999).

Conventional knowledge would tell us that people looking to avoid the negative emotions associated with a trauma would consume alcohol during the course of a traumatic event. However, a body of research indicated that this is not the case. Volpicelli, Ulm, and Hopson (1990), found that alcohol consumption typically increases following the trauma rather than during the trauma. They have termed this the *happy hour effect*.

As there has been a great deal of support for the happy hour effect in clinical research, it was postulated that the present unsolicited survey would indicate that executives on Wall Street would display significantly higher alcohol consumption rates during the postwar period of our time line rather than in anticipation of or during the actual invasion of Iraq by U.S. troops. It was also hypothesized that demographic categories such as marital status and annual income would be significantly related to problematic drinking behaviors as well.

Method

Participants

Participants were unsolicited individuals who visited a web site designed for brokers and other financial industry employees. Individuals who visited the web site were asked to complete a survey regarding their drinking behaviors. A total of 155 participants completed all or part of the demographics questionnaire and survey (see the results in the following section for specific information regarding participant demographics).

Materials

A demographics questionnaire and the AUDIT (Alcohol Use Disorders Identification Test; Babor et al., 1989) were used to collect data for the current study. The demographics questionnaire included questions regarding each participant's age, gender, marital status, state of residence, workplace residence, position, income level, and amount of exercise. These were all categorically presented to the participants, who chose the category most appropriate for them.

The AUDIT is a questionnaire that was developed to examine problematic drinking behaviors. This 10-item questionnaire examined drinking frequency, amount, the influence of drinking on daily living, and behaviors related to alcohol abuse. After completing the AUDIT, participants received feedback scores to help them understand the extent to which their drinking was impairing their lives. Scores were divided into categories labeled Very High, High, Moderate, Low, and No Problem, respectively. The web site located at catsg.com was used to post the demographics questionnaire and the AUDIT.

Design and Procedure

A survey was used to collect data to determine the demographic variables and the impact the war in Iraq had on drinking behavior. Respondents were first asked to read a thorough debriefing and informed consent page, which concluded with a prompt to click a button as a form of acceptance that they understood the benefits, limitations, and threats to their confidentiality. Immediately following this acceptance, the respondents were prompted to complete a demographics survey. Once this page was completed, the participants were asked to click on a button to move on to the AUDIT survey. At the conclusion of these items, participants received an overall AUDIT score and a narrative explaining any risks or problems with drinking that their score indicated. Referrals were made to substance abuse facilities throughout the United States if an individual felt that she needed help. At the end, data were analyzed using SPSS 8.0.

Results

Respondent Information

A total of 155 individuals responded to the current survey. Of the 155 respondents, 151 provided complete demographic data and answered all of the survey questions. The 151 respondents completing the demographic data and answering all of the survey questions were included in the current study. The four respondents who were not included left several demographic and questionnaire items blank. These respondents were deemed as inappropriate to include in the current study because a total score on the alcohol questionnaire could not be computed and because of their lack of demographic information. A sample of 151 participants was considered appropriate for all of the proposed analyses (that is, one-way ANOVA, correlations, t-tests).

Demographic Information of Respondents

Demographic information was collected regarding respondents' ages, gender, salary, marital status, amount of exercise per week, occupation, and residence. A summary of the participants' responses to questions regarding several demographic variables can be found in Table B.1.

Findings Regarding Hypotheses

One-way ANOVAs and post hoc analyses using t-tests for equality of means were conducted to examine the data collected from the current study. It was found that neither of the hypotheses were supported. The happy hour effect was not found to occur. In fact, significantly more problematic drinking behaviors occurred during the war than after the war in Iraq, $F = 4.13$, $p < .05$. When examining the total score on the AUDIT rating scale, the group of participants who completed the rating scale during the war had a significantly higher total score. Also, the prewar and during-war groups were not found to have significantly different amounts of problematic drinking behaviors. The additional hypothesis that specific demographic characteristics would relate to increased problematic drinking behaviors was also not supported. Unlike previous research, salary levels and marital status did not have a significant impact on drinking behavior in the current study.

Table B.1:   Participant Response

Demographic	Category	Number of Participants	Percent of Participants
Age	18–25	28	18%
	26–30	49	33%
	31–35	11	7%
	36–40	21	14%
	40–50	24	16%
	51+	18	12%
Gender	Female	25	17%
	Male	126	83%
Marital Status	Single	71	47%
	Married	55	36%
	Divorced	25	17%
Income Level	Under 50K	32	21%
	50K–100K	85	56%
	100K–150K	17	11%
	150K–200K	6	4%
	200K+	11	7%
Amount of Exercise per week	Not at all	40	27%
	<2 hours	59	39%
	2–4 hours	33	22%
	>4 hours	19	13%

The majority of the participants were found to be single men under the age of 30 who exercised infrequently and made less than $100,000 per year. Analysis of the additional demographic variables indicated that over 90 percent of the sample consisted of individuals working and living in and around Manhattan.

Findings Regarding Specific Drinking Behaviors on the AUDIT

Analyses were conducted to examine which specific problematic drinking behaviors were most significantly affected by being in the pre-, during-, or postwar groups. Interestingly, despite the finding that on average the problematic drinking behaviors of participants were highest during versus after the war when examining specific questions, there was only one area in which this was found to be marginally significant. How often participants drank was found to occur more frequently in the during-war than in the postwar group, $F = 2.46$, $p = .09$. Surprisingly, the during-war group was found to have more drinks containing alcohol on a typical day when they drank, $F = 6.83$,

$p < .01$, and binge drank more frequently, $F = 6.35$, $p < .01$, than the prewar group. Also, the during-war group indicated that they more frequently felt feelings of guilt or remorse after drinking than the prewar group, $F = 3.93$, $p < .05$.

Discussion

This preliminary investigation examined the issue of self-medication and coping skills during times of great stress and trauma, as evidenced by the aforementioned empirically validated research on alcohol use. Specifically, the investigators sought to illuminate whether individuals working within the financial services industry in New York City would display more problematic drinking behaviors after the conclusion of the war, thus supporting the happy hour effect pattern noted in the research of Volpicelli et al. (1999). Previous research by this investigator also indicated that these individuals typically use maladaptive coping skills for the purpose of relieving stress. Also, a long-standing cultural acceptance of drinking alcohol for the purposes of relaxing, conducting business meetings, and networking has existed on Wall Street. The findings of this investigation were noteworthy in that more of the problematic behaviors relating to alcohol use were reported during the war, as opposed to after major combat operations were concluded. This contradiction with prior research can be explained by various sociocultural factors and international events that may have interfaced with our target population before and at the time of this study.

Logic suggests that the events of September 11, 2001, would affect no group more significantly than the financial services executives working on Wall Street. Many individuals physically or vicariously witnessed the traumatic attack on the World Trade Center while others survived it. Many cases of Post-Traumatic Stress Disorder were reported within the first six months to a year after this event, as would be expected from an event that was so vivid and catastrophic in nature. Specifically, there appeared to be more instances of survivor guilt, startle responses, nightmares, depression, and insomnia as a consequence of this disaster. It was speculated that prescriptions for antidepressants had significantly increased in the New York City area and substance and alcohol use problems reportedly rose drastically as well.

Media depictions of this event registered with all Americans, but likely were more salient for New Yorkers who worked on Wall Street.

Graphic images of people jumping out of a burning building will probably never be forgotten by those who worked in close proximity to the World Trade Center. This was a time when Americans may have felt a strong sense of victimization and a loss of control. With each year since the September 11, 2001, anniversary, reactions appear to occur reliably, with the resurfacing of memorials and media coverage of the initial event that involved terrorism.

The findings that appear to contradict the happy hour effect may be stemming from the fact that many Wall Street workers have not fully recovered from the attacks on their security and way of life in 2001. This attack was viewed by many on Wall Street as a symbolic attack on corporate America and capitalism. When the United States officially announced it was going to attack Iraq using shock-and-awe tactics, many emotionally charged reactions were likely to be elicited for anyone who had lost a loved one, a colleague, or friend during this terrorist attack. It is not surprising that this group of individuals working within the financial services industry, a profession that has adopted alcohol use as an accepted means of socializing and conducting business, began drinking as a means of escaping these painful feelings during the attacks on Iraq. Historically, these individuals utilize maladaptive coping skills as evidenced by prior research conducted by the lead investigator who found that they reported using activities such as nightclubbing, masturbation, and drinking alcohol as a means of dealing with job stress. Demographic data indicated that the majority of the current sample spent less than two hours per week physically exercising as a means of dealing with their stress. Although this finding was not significantly related to an increase in problematic drinking behaviors, it supported prior research conducted by Cass et al. (2000), indicating that financial executives did not engage in healthy lifestyle habits.

Upon the initiation of war on Iraq, media coverage of the war spanned 24 hours a day and displayed vivid images of destruction and violence. Unlike previous war coverage, reporters were embedded in combat units, some incurring loss of life or injury. It is likely that the vivid imagery of the war, in conjunction with a reawakening of unresolved anger and guilt regarding the World Trade Center tragedy and maladaptive coping skills, may have led to the increase in problematic drinking behaviors during the war, rather than postwar, as noted in our findings. The findings that indicated higher levels of guilt and remorse for drinking and binge drinking in the during-war group is not surprising because of the likelihood that similar feelings of uncertainty, vulnerability, and guilt for experiencing painful emotions had resurfaced for individuals who find these feelings to be reprehensible. In many ways, New Yorkers have become habituated and desensitized to these vivid images of destruction and loss over the years, but more recent related events appear to bring their unresolved emotions to the surface quicker than they would be if a completely unrelated or shocking trauma were presented. Thus, the happy hour effect may still be applicable and accurate if a trauma is unrelated to any previous one.

Interestingly, it is speculated that the reasons why the prewar and during-war groups did not show significant differences in problematic drinking behaviors were because anticipation of war and war itself has historically had a positive impact on U.S. markets. Times of uncertainty, though (such as after the World Trade Center attack), historically lead to economic troubles in the United States and decimate the markets. Individuals who work as traders, analysts, or investment bankers felt some relief and hope for a struggling economy at the time the war was begun. Thus, it is likely that more market volatility existed in anticipation of war and during the war, which required that individuals working in the financial services arena needed to remain at work longer and behave in a more consistent fashion. The majority of participants experienced moderate problems related to their drinking as found by the AUDIT survey. It seems that had the prospect of war, or the actual ongoing war not existed, the sputtering economy and the bear market trends would have led to greater impairments as a result of drinking behaviors.

The secondary hypothesis regarding marital status and annual income and their relationship to alcohol use problems was not confirmed through our analysis. This may be due to factors such as having too few married participants included in the study and participants who were, on average, wealthier than would be expected if at high risk for having problematic drinking behaviors after experiencing a trauma.

The results of this investigation shed light on the importance of noticing the true casualties of Wall Street—the men and women who work within the highly stressful financial services industry. Specifically, it is imperative that corporate America begin to take alcohol and substance abuse seriously, because it has long-lasting and consequential effects on whole companies and individual employees' longevity within a firm.

Interventions like Exposure Response Prevention (ERP), support groups like Alcoholics Anonymous (AA) and Narcotics Anonymous (NA), and residential treatment for substance abuse problems are currently used as primary ways to deal with substance abuse concerns. ERP is based on the principles of operant and classical conditioning and is a way for an alcoholic to take back control over his addiction through the use of empowering self-statements and graduated exposure to the alcoholic product of his choice within a realistic context.

One must not forget that these individuals are constantly reminded of the horror of September 11th on a daily basis while walking to work. Internet studies and other support should continue to reach out to this highly reticent population of executives who hide behind a façade of confidence and strength for the purpose of not letting anyone know about their painful feelings or weaknesses. Financial executives will always fear that they will lose their jobs if they admit to a drinking problem, so it is important to continue research through the Internet for the purpose of helping these fearful individuals. Alcohol abuse is a tremendous problem that has been normalized by the culture of Wall Street and this study hopes to bring it back out in the spotlight. The current study hopes to aid future researchers in predicting alcohol use behaviors within this population if another tragedy or trauma should occur again.

A primary strength of this research design was the ability to tap into a specific target population of employees who could not be reached by handing out surveys within their work environment. The anonymity of using a home computer to fill out the survey instead of responding through a job-related one afforded us more honesty in the responses that we obtained. The AUDIT was, fortunately, usable within the public domain and is also a widely used instrument for assessing problematic drinking behaviors. Also, individuals with problematic drinking behaviors were provided with the awareness that they have a problem, along with strategies and referrals for resolving them.

Conversely, this study has limitations. A convenience sample that was collected from individuals who were drawn to our consulting firm's web site was used. Thus, anyone who was looking for help in the area of stress management or dealing with job burnout would be a likely respondent to this survey. This in itself may have superficially inflated the generalizability of our findings to the financial services industry as a whole. Also, while confidentiality was ensured in taking the survey, it is impossible to confirm the veracity of the responses given or the careers of the individuals who responded. Lastly, our sample was very homogeneous and rather small, which limits the generalizability of our findings. Future investigations should attempt to collect a larger sample of respondents, which include a wider variety of age ranges and marital statuses.

References

Brady, K.T., and Sonne, S.C. 1999. The role of stress in alcohol use, alcoholism treatment, and relapse. *Alcohol Research and Health*, 23(4):263–271.

Brown, G.R., and Anderson, B. 1991. Psychiatric morbidity in adult inpatients with childhood histories of sexual and physical abuse. *American Journal of Psychiatry*, 148:55–61.

Cass, A.M., Lewis, J., and Simco, E. 2000. "Casualties of Wall Street: An Assessment of the Walking Wounded." Directed Study Research, Nova Southeastern University.

Crum, R.M., Muntaner, C., Eaton, W.W., and Anthony, J.C. 1995. Occupational stress, and the risks of alcohol abuse and dependence. *Alcoholism: Clinical and Experimental Research*, 19:647–655.

Fullilove, M.T., Fullilove, R.E., Smith, M., Winkler, K., Micheal, C., Panzer, P.G., and Wallace, R. 1993. Violence, trauma, and post-traumatic stress disorder among women drug users. *Journal of Traumatic Stress*, 6:533–543.

Lex, B.W. 1991. Some gender differences in alcohol and polysubstance users. *Health Psychology*, 10:121–132.

Maier, S.F., and Seligman, M. 1976. Learned helplessness: Theory and evidence. *Journal of Experimental Psychology*, 105:3–46.

Najavits, L.M., Weiss, R.D., and Shaw, S.R. 1997. The link between substance abuse and post-traumatic stress disorder in women: A research review. *American Journal on Addictions*, 6(4):273–283.

Najavits, L.M., Weiss, R.D., and Shaw, S.R. 1999. A clinical profile of women with post-traumatic stress disorder and substance dependence. *Psychology of Addictive Behaviors*, 13(2):98–104.

Seeman, M., and Seeman, A.Z. 1992. Life strains, alienating, and drinking behavior. *Alcoholism: Clinical and Experimental Research*, 16:199–205.

Takeshita, T., Muruyama, S., and Morimoto, K. 1998. Relevance of both daily hassles and the ALDH2 genotype to problem drinking among Japanese male workers. *Alcoholism: Clinical and Experimental Research*, 22:115–120.

Volpicelli, J.R., Ulm, R.R., and Hopson, N. 1990. The bi-directional effects of shock on alcohol preference in rats. *Alcoholism: Clinical and Experimental Research*, 14:913–916.

Volpicelli, J.R., Balaraman, G., Hahn, J., Wallace, H., and Bux, D. 1999. The role of uncontrollable trauma in the development of PTSD and alcohol addiction. *Alcohol Research and Health*, 23(4):256–262.

Recommended Readings and Resources

Beck, Aaron T.; Rush, A. John; Shaw, Brian F.; Emery, Gary. *Cognitive Therapy of Depression*. The Guildford Press, 1987.

Burns, David D. *Feeling Good: The New Mood Therapy (Revised and Updated)*. Avon, 1999.

Copeland, Mary Ellen. *Living Without Depression & Manic Depression: A Workbook for Maintaining Mood Stability*. New Harbinger Publications, 1994.

Faupel, Adrian; Herrick, Elizabeth; Sharp, Peter. *Anger Management: A Practical Guide*. David Fulton Publishing, 1998.

Greenberger, Dennis and Padesky, Christine. *Mind Over Mood: Change How You Feel by Changing the Way You Think*. The Guildford Press, 1995.

Kassinove, Howard, Pd.D. *Anger Disorders: Definition, Diagnosis and Treatment*. Taylor & Francis, 1995.

Shaw, Brian F., Ph.D.; Ritvo, Paul, Ph.D.; Irvine, Jane, D.Phil.; Lewis, M. David. *Addiction & Recovery for Dummies*. John Wiley & Sons, 2004.

Rehabilitation Facilities

A.I.R. Alternatives
Alcohol and Drug Abuse Care Management
airalternatives.com

The Canyon
Depression, Anxiety, and Addiction
thecyn.com

Caron Foundation
Addictions
caron.org

Catalyst Support Services
Outpatient Case Management Services for Dual Diagnosis
catsg.com
catsg.com/support

Cirque Lodge
Addictions
cirquelodge.com

The Clinic at DuPont
Specialty Psychological and Psychiatric Services; Stress, Anxiety, Depression,
    Substance Abuse, Behavioral Health
theclinicatdupont.com

Betty Ford
Alcoholism
bettyfordcenter.org

Mountainside Treatment Center
Alcohol/Drug Addiction Treatment and Rehabilitation
mountainside.org

Sierra Tucson
Trauma/Addiction Treatment
sierratucson.com

SLS Health
Dual Diagnosis Residential Treatment
slshealth.com

Web Sites

nimh.nih.gov
National Institute of Mental Health

therapeuticresources.com
Therapeutic Resources, Inc.

depression-guide.com
Depression Guide, Inc.

catsg.com
Catalyst Strategies Group

nida.nih.gov
National Institute on Drug Abuse

Index

Printed in the United States
By Bookmasters